COMPREHENSION
to
GCSE

Geoff Barton

Oxford University Press

Oxford University Press, Great Clarendon Street, Oxford OX2 6DP

Oxford New York
Athens Auckland Bangkok Bogota
Buenos Aires Calcutta Cape Town Chennai
Dar es Salaam Delhi Florence Hong Kong
Istanbul Karachi Kuala Lumpur Madras Madrid
Melbourne Mexico City Mumbai Nairobi Paris
Singapore São Paulo Taipei Tokyo Toronto Warsaw

and associated companies in
Berlin Ibadan

Oxford is a trade mark of Oxford University Press

© Geoff Barton 1998
First published 1998

ISBN 0 19 831447 7

Printed in Italy

Contents

Introduction

Comprehension to GCSE has been written to help students do better in comprehension papers at GCSE. All Examination Boards require close attention to the reading of non-fiction and media texts. Comprehension-style questions at GCSE level tend to fall into two broad types:

1 NEAB-style questions

NEAB-style questions are broken down into sub-questions, each looking at a different aspect of the text in turn. Some will ask the student to select facts from the text, and so test straight 'factual' comprehension; other, more advanced questions ask the student to comment more broadly on the style, layout and language of the text or texts.

2 SEG-style questions

SEG sets questions of a different, more global kind – for instance, a single over-arching question may ask the student to compare and comment on two texts. Whilst these questions encourage students to give a fuller, perhaps more personal response, they can also appear dauntingly open-ended. SEG students need practice in learning how to structure their responses.

Preparing for GCSE

Amid a tightly-packed KS4 curriculum, with the pressures of coursework and set-texts, it can be tempting simply to dish out past papers as a way of preparing students for the non-fiction requirements of the final examination. Whilst this process is important and useful, it does not explicitly teach students the skills they will need to succeed.

The experience of most English teachers, therefore, is that comprehension is a reading skill which needs to be actively taught. But how to find the time and – more pressing – where to find the resources? *Comprehension to GCSE* has been written with the intention of supporting this important dimension of GCSE preparation – by providing active teaching approaches to develop students' comprehension skills in response to both models of comprehension questions.

NEAB: The *Comprehension to GCSE* Students' Book provides a range of questions in the NEAB style; the accompanying Answer Book provides sample answers to those questions.

SEG: The Answer Book includes extra, SEG-style questions to accompany the texts in the Students' Book, plus advice points to help students structure their responses.

The Students' Book

Key features

This book contains a range of non-fiction texts from a variety of genres. Whereas in *Comprehension to 14* we included drama, poetry and fiction texts, here we concentrate on the kinds of texts students will encounter in, for example, Paper 1 of the NEAB examination and Papers 5 and 7 of the SEG examination. The activities therefore provide useful practice in their own right. But, conscious that students are not always clear about what they need to do to make tangible improvements, we have included a variety of teaching strategies to help improve students' grades.

Organization by genre

The organization of the book is by genre: this is important for developing students' sensitivity to the way language is used differently in different types of writing. The introduction to each unit exemplifies the stylistic features of different genres.

Reading and writing questions

The majority of the sections of the Students' Book contain
- a Foundation-level text plus reading questions – labelled A
- a Higher-level text plus reading questions – labelled B
- at least one writing question – 'Writing to argue, persuade or instruct' – which asks students to re-present information from the original texts in a different form.

The reading questions are designed particularly to prepare students working towards the NEAB papers; however, their format also provides good groundwork for students who will later need to move on to a broader (SEG-style) model of question.

Annotations

But this isn't simply a collection of texts and questions. Most noticeable is the inclusion of annotations within most spreads – guidelines for students to help them towards the kinds of language points they might make. This isn't making the task easier: it is making it more focused and teaching students how, in the final exam, they should be tackling questions. The annotations are integral to the learning model of the book.

Grammar

Grammar is a central feature of *Comprehension to GCSE*. A greater emphasis on grammar at KS3 and KS4 has here been reflected in reading questions which encourage analysis of linguistic structure – with specific guidance on how to respond to such questions. Students often find this part of comprehension the most difficult – precisely what to say about the vocabulary and grammar. And yet these are the areas which can help students to achieve their highest marks.

The approach here is to encourage students to notice how grammatical features vary according to genre: the kinds of sentences you find in autobiographies are not necessarily the same as the kinds of sentences in instructional writing, for example. The advice panels and annotations continually nudge students towards more explicit recognition of this.

Differentiation

The organization of texts according to their accessibility (A – Foundation-level texts; B – Higher-level texts) provides a number of possibilities. You can use the texts to assist in differentiation within a mixed ability class – some students working on text A, some on text B; or you can see text A as developing the skills which can then be assessed at a higher level with text B. Both approaches work well.

The Answer Book

Sample answers – plus annotations

The Answer Book not only includes a breakdown of the points students may offer as answers, but also some sample answers for students to look at. The idea here is that you might photocopy the answers and encourage students to interrogate them.

The answers are annotated to show their strengths and weaknesses, and our hope is that students' responses to non-fiction will be significantly enhanced through studying them. The annotations to questions in the Students' Book; the sample answers and annotations in the Answer Book – both of these are designed to teach students skills which are too often left implicit.

In addition, the Answer Book also includes further, broader, comparison-based questions in the style of SEG Papers 5 and 7; and Self-Help Sheets to support the writing activities in the Students' Book.

Conclusion

I hope that students will find much here to inform and entertain them. It is a book to be enjoyed as well as serving an important teaching purpose. It should prove a time-saver in the classroom

– providing you with texts, questions, guidance, and sample answers for students of all abilities.

Most of all I hope that the comprehension skills of your students – still integral to success at GCSE – will be significantly enhanced. These skills are too important to leave to chance, or to a diet of past papers. I therefore hope that the reassuring and systematic approach of *Comprehension to GCSE* proves highly successful with your students.

Geoff Barton

Leaflets

Leaflets have different purposes. Some are designed to inform – to give you information. Others aim to entertain you. Most are also designed to persuade you to do something. They might persuade you to buy a product, or to change your opinion about an issue, or to support a campaign.

During your GCSE course you will be expected to read and respond to leaflets; notice the way they use layout and language to achieve their effect; and you may be asked to create a leaflet of your own – possibly under exam conditions.

Skills checklist

Reading leaflets
- Show you can understand what is in the leaflet.
- Comment on the way the leaflet is written and designed.
- Make points about the use of language to get the highest marks.

Writing leaflets
- Write for a specific audience (e.g. a certain age group).
- Inform and sometimes persuade your readers.
- Use layout to help communicate your message.

Language features

To gain higher grades at GCSE you'll need to be able to discuss the language of leaflets. Look out for:

- short paragraphs (to help you to absorb information quickly)
- a straightforward written style (to be clear)
- dramatic vocabulary (to get your attention)
- bullet-points (to keep the style snappy)
- facts and statistics (to encourage you to believe what is being said)
- slogans (to help you to remember the message)
- quotations (to make you think that other people support the idea).

Advice panel

- Get used to the way leaflets work. Pick them up in supermarkets, shops, the doctor's waiting-room.
- Make some notes on layout ideas you could use (use of headings, sub-headings, images, slogans ...).
- Remember that to get a higher grade you'll need to comment on the language the writer uses – just making points about the layout won't be enough.
- When looking at language you might think about: typical words, lengths of sentences, whether the style is informal, personal, serious or humorous, and so on.
- When creating a leaflet in an exam, don't spend too long on the design of your leaflet. Just sketch ideas and label what they should look like. You'll get most marks for your use of language.

Just £3 a month will help rescue more animals like Trio

Trio's Story

When Trio made a mess in the bedroom, his owner saw red.

Any responsible, caring owner would have expected it from a puppy that's just four months old. But Trio's owner lost his temper.

He grabbed Trio round the belly, squeezing him so tight he began to cry out. To Trio's owner, that meant the dog knew he'd misbehaved. So to punish him, he threw Trio across the room with full force, smashing him against a cupboard.

Petrified and terribly injured, the puppy crawled away and hid under a cot.

When Trio's owner finally realised how seriously injured he was, he took him to the police station and claimed he was a stray!

Trio's leg was so badly damaged we had to amputate. But with the loving attentions of RSPCA staff, Trio soon recovered and now he's living in a happy new home. His cruel owner has been prosecuted and banned from keeping animals for five years.

Photo: *Sunday Mirror*

Dear Friend

As an RSPCA inspector, I've dedicated my life to animals. I'm regularly on call 24 hours a day, ready to rescue animals like Trio at a moment's notice.

Every year the RSPCA uncovers even more cases of the most appalling cruelty and now, more than ever before, we need your help.

In just one year we rescued 6,982 abused and neglected animals.

I can't turn my back on all the battered, tormented and abandoned animals who need my help. Will you give me the resources I need to fight this rising tide of cruelty?

Just £3 a month will help rescue many more animals in torment and give them the love and care they so desperately need. Please, make your monthly Standing Order today.

Thank you for giving animals like Trio another chance.

C. Strong

Inspector Colin Strong

Just one day old and your owner doesn't want you.

So what does he do? Simply flushes you down the toilet. It's hard to believe, but that's just what happened to Poppy.

Only the sharp ears of a neighbour who heard Poppy's whimpers as she was swept along the drain pipe saved her from certain death. The RSPCA and the Fire Brigade were called, and after two hours of frantic digging through a patio and five feet of earth, we finally reached the petrified, half-drowned pup. Poppy was taken to the RSPCA's Barnes Hill hospital where she was given just a 50-50 chance of survival. Devoted care around the clock pulled Poppy back from the brink and she's now been found a new home with responsible owners.

It takes weeks of neglect to reduce a healthy dog to the pathetic sight you see here. Tara was so weak when we rescued her that she couldn't even struggle to her feet.

The vet said Tara was very close to death, but with weeks of tender, expert care she made a full recovery.

 We receive no government funding

Your support helps to pay for...

- Life-saving first aid and essential medication for rescued animals.
- Expert veterinary care in RSPCA centres, hospitals and clinics.
- Our 24-hour emergency service, answering over a million calls for help every year.
- 305 RSPCA inspectors providing cover 24 hours a day, all year round.

If you would prefer to send a donation, make your cheque or postal order payable to: **RSPCA**. Send your donations, along with your name and address to: **RSPCA, FREEPOST, BRISTOL BS38 7LQ.** NO STAMP NEEDED – but if you use one, more of our funds go to help animals. Please do not use this address to report cruelty – call our National Helpline on **0990 555999** (National rates will apply.)

Make your monthly Standing Order today

Reading

A RSPCA leaflet

The leaflet opposite is produced by the Royal Society for the Prevention of Cruelty to Animals (RSPCA). Read it carefully and think about:

- what its main message is
- who it is aimed at
- what it tries to persuade readers to do.

A

1 Name one thing that donations to the RSPCA might help to pay for. (2 marks)

2 At the foot of the leaflet it says 'We receive no government funding'. Why do you think it says this? (2 marks)

3 Write two sentences using your own words. In one, say what happened to Trio. In the other, say what happened to Poppy. (4 marks)

B

4 Look at the letter from Inspector Colin Strong in the centre of the leaflet. What impression do you get of him? (6 marks)

Advice

You might look at the photograph of him – why is he shown holding an animal? What do we learn about his commitment to the job?

What impression does he give when he says, 'I can't turn my back on ...'? Why do you think the letter is signed by him personally?

5 How does the leaflet persuade readers to support the work of the RSPCA? You might comment upon:

- the layout
- the content
- the language. (6 marks)

Advice

You might show how the **layout** uses different types of text – Trio's story; a letter; a shaded panel showing where your money goes; plus emotional photographs. You might comment on the way the **content** includes several stories, about Trio, Poppy and Tara; also we are encouraged to get to know Inspector Strong. This is an emotional approach – getting the reader involved. Why?
You might comment on the violent **language** – 'grabbed', 'squeezing', 'smashing'. Why do you think these words are used? You might mention the short paragraphs and fairly short sentences. You might comment on the personal tone of the letter addressed 'Dear Friend'.

HELP KEEP GREENPEACE CAMPAIGNERS IN ACTION

When a group of Canadians sailed their small boat into a nuclear test zone in 1971, Greenpeace was born.

This group of protesters had found a way of forcing decision-makers to take notice. They had also captured the imagination of a generation who could see the urgent need for action to save the planet.

ACTION MAKES THE WORLD LISTEN

Today – only two decades later – Greenpeace is working right around the world to save rainforests, avert global warming, oppose toxic pollution and confront nuclear folly.

Scaling chimneys that pump out toxic emissions, wading through effluent that contains deadly chemicals to block pipelines ... our campaigners will do whatever it takes to alert government and industry to the risks the world faces.

ACTION WINS VICTORY FOR THE ENVIRONMENT

Non-violent direct action is our unique way of exposing environmental crime. It creates headline news. And makes

guilty parties clean up their act, under heavy public pressure. The following examples are proof:

ACTION in the high seas stopped Japanese tuna fishermen using giant drift nets that killed hundreds of thousands of dolphins.

ACTION blocked the effluent pipe of chemical giant Albright and Wilson which spewed toxic pollution into the Irish Sea, and, helped by a successful Greenpeace prosecution, cut the discharge by 95%.

ACTION shielding thousands of baby harp seal pups from hunters on the east coast of Canada, helped put an end to their commercial trade in seal fur.

And **ACTION** is what we invite you to take today.

We're NOT asking you to sail under falling barrels of nuclear waste or to stand between harpoon and whale. All we ask is that you support us – by joining Greenpeace today.

GREENPEACE CAMPAIGNS

Join us NOW and help influence the following campaigns:

GLOBAL WARMING – we've alerted policy-makers to measures they must adopt to stop temperatures rising to levels never before felt by humans on earth.

RAINFORESTS – we're acting within rainforest countries to stop the destruction that threatens to wipe out all forests within our own lifetimes.

WHALING – we'll continue to match our inflatables against whalers, such as the Norwegians who resume commercial whaling from January 1993.

OZONE – our demand for an immediate ban on ozone-depleting chemicals will continue to put pressure on polluters like ICI and Du Pont.

ACTION SPEA LOUDE

Text B

GREENPEACE IN ACTION
AINST THE WHALERS

PLANET EARTH IS 4,600 MILLION YEARS OLD

At the stern of a whaling ship, protesters in two tiny Greenpeace boats stopped whales being hauled aboard.

Despite being pelted with icy water from the ship's fire hoses, they drove in close to the slipway and tied up. The ship's crew lowered a grappling hook. The hook caught the rope tying up one of the boats – and in a highly dangerous act, the ship's crew winched it in.

The tiny Greenpeace boat was lifted almost vertically before the ship's crew cut the rope – sending it crashing back down into the water. Its engines cut out on impact.

This action, part of a two month protest against 'scientific' whaling' in Antarctica, *saved one whale for every day spent at sea* – and put whaling back on the public agenda.

This one example sums up what Greenpeace is about: TAKING ACTION to stop the destruction of the natural world.

So join us now – because in the fight to save this fragile planet, Greenpeace proves that ACTIONS SPEAK LOUDER.

If we condense this inconceivable time-span into an understandable concept, we can liken the Earth to a person of 46 years of age.

Nothing is known about the first 7 years of this person's life, and whilst only scattered information exists about the middle span, we know that only at the age of 42 did the Earth begin to flower.

Dinosaurs and the great reptiles did not appear until one year ago, when the planet was 45. Mammals arrived only 8 months ago; in the middle of last week, human-like apes evolved into ape-like humans, and at the weekend the last ice age enveloped the Earth.

Modern humans have been around for four hours. During the last hour, we discovered agriculture. The industrial revolution began a minute ago.

During those sixty seconds of biological time, humans have made a rubbish tip of Paradise.

We have caused the extinction of many hundreds of animal species, ransacked the planet for fuel and now stand like brutish infants, gloating over this meteoric rise to ascendancy, on the brink of the final mass extinction and of effectively destroying this oasis of life in the solar system.

GREENPEACE

Reading

 Greenpeace leaflet

The leaflet on pages 14 and 15 was produced by the environmental pressure group, Greenpeace. Read it through and think about:

- what it aims to achieve
- who it might be aimed at.

A

1 How did the Greenpeace organization begin? (1 mark)

2 Name two issues that Greenpeace campaigns about. (1 mark)

3 In the description of the campaign against whaling, the leaflet says that Greenpeace 'put whaling back on the public agenda'. Say, in your own words, what you think this means. (2 marks)

B

4 The last page of the leaflet gives a brief history of the planet Earth. What point is this passage of text making? (4 marks)

Advice

Talking about the Earth as millions of years old can seem unreal and difficult to comprehend. Think about what the writer is trying to achieve here.

5 Look more closely at the design of the leaflet. Write a paragraph about the use of:

 images
- headlines
- subheadings.

How successful is the layout in grabbing and holding the reader's attention? (6 marks)

Advice

Images: you might comment that they are mostly action shots – what does this show about Greenpeace? They show a variety of different campaigns – why, do you think?
Headlines: look at the words 'campaigners' and 'in action'. What impression does this create of the people involved?

Subheadings: why all the repetition of 'action'? When talking about how successful the layout is, you might comment on why the images were chosen – is their purpose always clear? Is the design easy to read or cluttered?

6 Does the language of the leaflet seem straightforward or difficult? Is it simple or high-level? Which parts are easiest to follow and which cause difficulty? Write a brief paragraph commenting on the language of the leaflet.

(6 marks)

Advice

Look at the type of words used: 'toxic emissions', 'effluent', 'ozone'. Could the writer have used simpler words and, if so, what would the effect have been? What do these complex, technical words tell you about the audience for the leaflet - the readers it is aimed at?

Do you find the tone formal or informal? Look at words like 'we're' and the frequent use of 'we' and 'you'.

Writing to argue, persuade or instruct

A RSPCA leaflet

The RSPCA leaflet says, 'We receive no government funding'. Imagine that after reading about the work of the RSPCA you write to the Government to say that you think they should help to support the RSPCA. Use the information from the leaflet to show the work the RSPCA does. Quote some of the facts and use some of the examples. Make your letter as persuasive as possible.

Write your letter to:

Ms A. Crowther
Funding Minister
Whitehall
London

Advice

For practical advice on writing your letter, see Self-Help Sheets 4 and 5 in the Answer Book.

To look at different types of letters, see pages 109-118.

B Greenpeace leaflet

Imagine you have just joined Greenpeace to work on their advertising campaigns. Write a memo to the Director of Marketing saying what you think of their current leaflet – what works and what doesn't, and how you might improve it.

Comment on the layout, the language, and the message. Set out your memo like this:

MEMO

From: Your name
To: Alex Crabbe, Marketing Director

Date:

Advice   For practical advice on writing memos, see Self-Help Sheet 6 in the Answer Book.

Leaflets comparison

Introduction

Read the two leaflets *Healthy Eating for Children* (text A) and *Eating and Good Health* (text B) on the following pages. The first was produced by Tesco, the other by Waitrose.

Comparison

Healthy Eating leaflets

1 What reasons do the two leaflets give to persuade us to think more about our diets? **(4 marks)**

2 Write down three facts you learn from the leaflets. Then write down three pieces of advice you learn. **(6 marks)**

3 Compare the two leaflets and describe what you notice about:

- who they are aimed at
- what they say
- how they are set out
- the language they use.

(10 marks)

Text A

Healthy Eating For

Children

FOOD
ADVICE
SERVICE

at
TESCO

262

Text A

tips

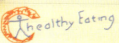
Healthy Eating

1. Only buy the foods you want your children to eat. Then let them make their own choices from the careful selection you provide.

2. Encourage children to get involved in planning and preparing meals e.g. For example children who help make their packed lunches are more likely to eat them.

3. Set an example by eating the right foods and having regular meal times. Make all meal times an occasion and avoid distractions such as television.

4. Make foods attractive and fun.

5. If your child doesn't like vegetables, try to disguise them in other foods e.g. soups, stews, moussaka.

6. Always grill food, especially meat products like sausages and burgers, choose the low-fat ones. Trim any excess fat from meat before cooking.

7. Unsalted nuts and raisins make ideal snacks for school lunch boxes.

8. Purée fresh, canned or frozen fruit and stir into yogurt or fromage frais for an easy dessert.

9. Make your own fish cakes using canned fish (such as tuna) and mashed potato. Don't forget to add an extra vegetable such as sweetcorn.

10. Give your children fruit for snacks instead of sweets. Choose smaller fruits such as small bananas, tangerines or small bunches of grapes. Make up a mini fruit basket for them, so they can make the choice themselves.

The Healthy Eating Guide For Children is one in a series of leaflets. For any advice on food and health write to: The Food Advice Service, Tesco Stores Ltd, P.O. Box 18, Cheshunt, Herts EN8 9SL. © Tesco Stores Ltd.

Text A

STARTING YOUNG

Eating healthily is important for children. They need large amounts of calories and nutrients to meet their energy needs, for repair and maintenance and to fuel growth. Developing good eating habits in children early on will mean they are more likely to eat healthily as they grow up and reduce the risk of developing coronary heart disease and other illnesses in later life.

Healthy eating for young children is not the same as for adults. Children have smaller stomachs than adults, so they need smaller more regular meals. They also need more concentrated forms of calories and nutrients to make up a well-balanced diet.

This doesn't mean they can't have low-fat or reduced-fat products or fibre-providing foods. But they should not have too much of either of these.

FATS

While children shouldn't have a very low-fat diet, the balance of fats should be the same as for adults, cutting down on saturated fats in favour of unsaturated ones.

It is recommended that children under two years old have full-fat milk, but after that they can have semi-skimmed if the calories and nutrients are supplied by other sources in a healthy, varied diet. Skimmed milk can be introduced from the age of five.

SUGARS & TEETH

Children's teeth are most at risk from tooth decay, so try and avoid too many sweets, especially the sticky, chewy ones. Keep sweets and chocolates for meal times only - banning them altogether does not usually work. Dilute fruit juices or give them milk or fizzy water to drink. Make sure they brush their teeth after eating sweets and have a good dental care routine. Your dentist can give you more details.

VITAMINS & MINERALS

A good variety of foods should ensure children get all the vitamins and minerals they need. Iron is important for young children. Meat and dark-green vegetables are rich sources of iron. It is also found in bread, eggs, nuts and lentils.

Calcium and Vitamin D are important for growing children. Milk, cheese and yogurt are good sources of calcium (even low-fat varieties). It is also found in white bread, the soft bones of fish, e.g. canned sardines, and pulses such as baked beans. Vitamin D is found in foods like liver, oily fish and eggs. It is also made in the body by the action of sunlight on the skin.

Text B

EATING & GOOD HEALTH

WAITROSE

food shops of the John Lewis Partnership

MEETING THE
THE **HEALTH** OF THE **NATION**
CHALLENGE

It makes sense to eat the food which provides us with all the nutrients our bodies need – but what exactly is a balanced diet? Which foods contribute most to our well-being? Should we avoid certain foods altogether?

This plate has been designed to help you plan a healthy diet. It is based on 'The Balance of Good Health' produced by the Department of Health, the Ministry of Agriculture, Fisheries and Food and the Health Education Authority.

FRUIT AND VEGETABLES

It is recommended that we eat at least five portions of fruit and vegetables every day, approximately 1lb(450g) in total. These are the foods which provide us with the fibre, minerals and essential vitamins which keep our bodies in good working order. Fresh, frozen, canned and dried fruit and vegetables are all available at Waitrose.

Always remember 5 a day.

MEAT, FISH AND ALTERNATIVES

All kinds of seafood, red and white meats, eggs, nuts, beans and pulses fall into this group. They are important elements of a healthy diet because they contain protein, vitamins and minerals. Enjoy them in moderate amounts and look for lower fat alternatives – lean cuts of meat or skinless chicken fillets. It is recommended that two portions of fish are eaten each week, one of which should be an oily variety like mackerel.

FOODS CONTAINING FAT. FOODS CONTAINING SUGAR

Cakes, biscuits, sweets, crisps and many drinks fall into this group. As they contain large quantities of fat, sugar and salt, they should only be eaten occasionally and in small amounts. Opt for low fat spreads, low sugar drinks and reduced calorie mayonnaise and dips.

BREAD, CEREALS AND POTATOES

These provide us with energy, starch, fibre, vitamins and minerals. The group includes rice and pasta. Try to eat a wide variety and pick wholemeal, wholegrain and brown alternatives for extra fibre.

MILK AND DAIRY PRODUCTS

Calcium, protein and important vitamins such as A and D are found in milk and dairy products. Enjoy them in moderation and try lower fat options such as skimmed and semi-skimmed milk, low fat yogurts and reduced fat cheeses. Babies and young children should always be given full fat milk and dairy products as they contain essential nutrients for early growth.

Text B

A BALANCING ACT

To balance your diet, simply try to enjoy a wide variety of different foods in the proportions shown on the plate. What you will find is that, far from being restrictive, it will encourage you to be more adventurous when planning your daily meals.

HOW WAITROSE CAN HELP

We aim to make it as simple as possible for you to eat well by providing plenty of choice in all our branches and including an easy reference nutrition panel on most Waitrose products. This tells you how much energy – shown as kiloJoules or kilocalories – protein, carbohydrate and fat is present in 100g of that food. On some packaging, the amount of sugars, saturates, fibre and sodium is also shown.

NUTRITION INFORMATION TYPICAL VALUES

	PER 100g	PER PACK
Energy	526kJ	2104kJ
	125kcal	500kcal
Protein	2.5g	10.0g
Carbohydrate	15.8g	63.2g
of which sugars	3.8g	15.2g
Fat	5.8g	23.2g
of which saturates	0.8g	3.2g
Fibre	1.4g	5.6g
Sodium	0.4g	1.7g

Number of calories per 100g — (Energy 125kcal)

Total sugars per 100g — (of which sugars)

Total amount of fat per 100g — (Fat)

COUNTING THE CALORIES

Calories provide us with energy. The number you need each day will depend on your age, gender and lifestyle.

Age: The amount of energy we require diminishes with age, so adolescents need more calories than mature adults.

Gender: Generally speaking, women need fewer calories than men.

Lifestyle: The more active your lifestyle, the more calories your diet should include. If you are overweight, it suggests you are eating too many calories for your daily needs, and you should consider reducing your intake.

Reportage

Introduction

Reportage is a term used to describe the way events are reported. The root of the word is Latin, *reportare*, meaning 'to carry back', so a reporter is someone who carries back news. Often we think of these people as journalists – people who view an event, like a trial, a crash, or a concert, and then write about or talk about what they have seen.

Journalism is one form of reportage – and, as this book shows, there are a variety of styles of newspaper journalism, with different purposes and audiences. But reportage can also mean eyewitness accounts – when people who are not trained journalists say what they saw; or writers describe events in essays and diaries, perhaps just for themselves rather than for a media audience.

For example, a journalist will usually use the first sentence to tell you the whole story in brief:

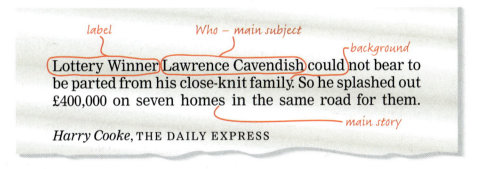

label — Who – main subject — background

Lottery Winner Lawrence Cavendish could not bear to be parted from his close-knit family. So he splashed out £400,000 on seven homes in the same road for them.

main story

Harry Cooke, THE DAILY EXPRESS

A different style of reportage might tell the story in a different way:

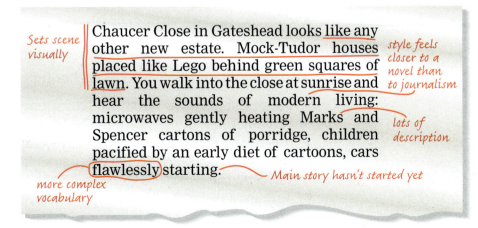

Sets scene visually

Chaucer Close in Gateshead looks like any other new estate. Mock-Tudor houses placed like Lego behind green squares of lawn. You walk into the close at sunrise and hear the sounds of modern living: microwaves gently heating Marks and Spencer cartons of porridge, children pacified by an early diet of cartoons, cars flawlessly starting.

style feels closer to a novel than to journalism

lots of description

Main story hasn't started yet

more complex vocabulary

This unit shows you the difference between two forms of reportage, both on the theme of hunting. Text A is an example of journalism: Lynne Wallis of the *Daily Express* joins a fox hunt and describes what she sees. Text B is a more personal account by the writer George Orwell. While working as a police officer in Burma, near India, Orwell watches the death of an elephant. He describes what he sees – not for a newspaper audience, but almost as if it is the only way to cope with what he has witnessed.

Skills checklist

Reading reportage

- Look at the writer's style – is it journalistic, fast-moving, dramatic? Or reflective, thoughtful, and serious?
- Examine the way events are described – for example, neutrally, or with fascination, disgust or delight.
- Find evidence of who the text is aimed at and what its purpose is.

Writing reportage

- Describe an event in detail to make the reader feel she is there with you.
- Structure your account to create the most powerful effect.
- Choose a style which is most appropriate to your purpose and audience.

Language features

To gain higher grades at GCSE you'll need to be able to discuss the language of reportage. Look out for the key features of journalism:

- layout: headlines, sub-headings, short paragraphs (all designed to hold our attention)
- language: dramatic vocabulary ('crisis', 'bid', 'drama', 'disaster') to make us interested
- content: finding stories containing conflict (to add to the feeling of drama)

Also look out for the features of other reportage styles:

- use of the personal pronoun 'I' to show the writer was actually there at the event
- precise details of where and when something happened, perhaps a lot of descriptive writing, to help the reader to visualize the scene
- perhaps a more emotional style than we expect to find in journalism – showing us what the writer thinks and how she is reflecting on the impact of events.

Advice panel • • • • • • • • • • • • •

- Read a range of reportage: look at different newspaper reports of the same events.
- Look at the way writers structure their stories – you don't have to start with what happened first and then describe it in order.
- Listen to television and radio journalism to learn more about the way journalists under pressure tell stories in as few words as possible.
- Read more examples of non-journalistic reportage in John Carey, *The Faber Book of Reportage*, John E. Lewis, *Eyewitness: The Twentieth Century* and the excellent magazine, *Granta*.

Reading

A **Newspaper report**

This text comes from the *Daily Express*. It tries to describe the different types of people who are involved in fox-hunting – the hunters and the hunt monitors. As you read, look at:

- what impression it gives of hunters and hunt monitors
- whether the article seems factual or based upon opinion
- what you can work out about the writer's opinion.

Different classes who are brought together by the thrill of the chase

Arguments over hunting will become even fiercer when a Bill to ban it receives its second Commons reading shortly. LYNNE WALLIS *rode with the hounds and ran with protesters to hear both sides.*

LIFE AND TIMES

Roderick Moore, joint master of the New Forest Hunt, is spruced up in hacking jacket, pristine breeches and a pair of £300 'mahogany top' riding boots. 'Come up to the flesh wagon to see your horse,' he says. 'The vehicle bringing the hounds has broken down, I'm afraid. Might be a bit of a wait.'

Roderick, 27, is not the sort who would set a filly's heart on fire in Jilly Cooper's riding novels. He is married to Arabella and they are both barristers in Southampton. They met through hunting, hunted on the morning of their wedding and had a fox iced on to their wedding cake. 'This is the ideal hobby for us,' says Arabella.

It's 7.10 am on Saturday. About 20 people are waiting for the off. As I mount Tonka, ladies in foxy ties and hairnets lead their mounts expertly around the field. Their backs are ramrod straight, their faces set – perhaps in anticipation of thrills and kills ahead.

The horses are getting frisky. Marilyn Husbands, a girlish fortysomething who runs a chain of women's dress shops, is keen to emphasize that hunting isn't a 'class thing'. She says (three times): 'I'm terribly ordinary.' Someone else remarks how egalitarian the New Forest Hunt is. 'What's that mean, then?' asks Marilyn.

The hounds arrive and we set off. To my surprise, my mount, which I had been assured was gentle and slow, goes into a fast canter at the front of the hunt. I am okay for 15 minutes and then lose balance (to cries of 'Oh no, she's fallen orf'). I give in and follow the hunt for the rest of the day in a jeep driven by one of the 'foot' followers.

There is lots of barking and yelping, but it leads nowhere. Christopher Lawrence-Price, who drives down from London for the hunt, tells me: 'The foxes really are clever. The scent comes from their feet and they will run through smelly areas with ferns or cattle to put the hounds off the scent. We don't actually catch all that many.'

The tiny number of foxes killed and the 'classlessness' of the hunt are recurring themes. It's 10.15 am, and there's no sniff of a chase. Antonia Johnson, a groom from the stables, is trying to control an excitable horse. She says: 'I've hunted from when I was little. Now, all my friends are anti but they just don't understand. I hate it when people make snap decisions about hunting without knowing anything about it.'

Someone says: 'They're drawing to the right' and the riders head off, leaving Keith Colbert wondering whether his skills will be called upon. Keith, an electrician from Poole, is a 'terrier man'. His job is to put his terrier underground to capture foxes but, the law says, only if a farmer has a nuisance fox he wants killed. The terrier is restless; so is Keith: 'She's dying to go down and see some action, and to be honest, I am too.' But his services are redundant, this Saturday at least. He is 'gutted'.

After the meet, as brandy, gin, coffee and bacon sandwiches are served, the hunt's secretary Diana Moore tells me she has never refused anyone entry. She even has a plumber from Tottenham on board. Diana insists: 'The camaraderie is so good here, it really doesn't matter if you're a dustman or a duke, a lady or a lollipop lady, everyone is welcome.'

There is a lollipop lady – Penny Rendle – and she says: 'What makes it so exciting is that you never know where you're going to end up. I live for it, for the buzz, the adrenaline, and such nice people.'

Right, wrong, nice or nasty, I'm still disappointed that I didn't hear one single 'Tally Ho!' all day.

FOXED: The hunt finds itself on the wrong scent.

In hot pursuit, saboteurs on the hunt's trail

FOUR OF the hunt monitors, affiliated to The League Against Cruel Sports, arrive in a battered old vehicle and park just yards from where the huntsmen are mounting. As long as they're visible, they say, the hunt can't break the rules.

Daphne Rickerts, 46, mother of three adolescent daughters, drives a Range Rover and wears a Barbour. She looks as if she belongs on the other side. A former employee of the Inland Revenue, Daphne became involved in the anti-hunt movement a few years ago. 'I saw a pack of dogs chasing hares and ripping them to pieces, just 20 yards from my home.'

The hunt sets off through dense woodland. Frankie Horan, a nurse in her 50s, follows as closely as possible by car and relays locations by radio to the others, speaking in code to foil unwanted listeners.

Frankie met Ken James, her seventysomething partner, through the League. Ken spent his career as a draughtsman in the aircraft industry but these days he prefers to watch wildlife,

MONITORS: protesters keep a sharp eye out.

earning himself the nickname Badger.

Ken and Daphne once took the hunt to court, after a 'terrier man' put an injured terrier back down a hole to get a fox out. 'We got him done for cruelty because we had it all on video,' says Ken, triumphantly.

Frankie, Ken and Daphne get news via radio, from sister and brother team Rachel and Peter White, that the hunt is up at the nearby Eyeworth Lodge and they arrive to find a handful of riders desperately trying to keep the hounds together. The hunt Master is conspicuously absent.

'He's lost his hunt and his hounds,' says Daphne, laughing.

The others begin to mock the huntsmen, and suddenly the horse beneath a portly man starts to buck. He gives it a swift lash with his riding crop, to the startled cries of the monitors. The atmosphere is tense.

There is no kill that morning. The monitors, clearly exhausted, are happy about that. 'But there's so much to be done,' says Frankie. Ken, packing his pipe, adds wistfully: 'We'll never get a perfect world while humans are in it.'

The Daily Express, 4 November 1997

Word bank

Barbour   make of waxed coat worn in the countryside
egalitarian   equal
pristine   very clean

A

1 Why do Roderick and Arabella have a fox iced onto their wedding cake?   (2 marks)

2 What evidence is there that foxes are clever?   (2 marks)

3 Why did Daphne Rickerts first join the League Against Cruel Sports?   (2 marks)

B

4 The headline to the article is, 'Different classes who are brought together by the thrill of the chase'. Write a paragraph about some of the different types of people who are involved in fox-hunting – as hunters and as hunt monitors.   (6 marks)

Advice

You need to look at the backgrounds of the people involved – what do they actually do for a living? One of the hunters says, 'It doesn't really matter if you're a dust-man or a duke, a lady or a lollipop lady…'. Look to see if there is such a range of people. See if the kind of people who are hunt monitors come from very different backgrounds. You might also look at the names of the participants. Do these give any hints about the background of the people? In your last sentence, try to say whether there is a variety of different classes (as it says in the headline), or whether the range is actually quite narrow.

5 Is the writer of the article neutral, or does she seem to be on the side of either the hunters or hunt monitors? Support your response with specific examples. (8 marks)

Advice

Look at the way the hunt is described. Is it exciting and glamorous? Or is it depicted as chaotic and poorly organized? Are the hunters shown as basically pleasant people who are just there to enjoy themselves? Or does the writer make them seem cruel, rather dim, or just unfeeling?

Are there any hints that the hunters are trying to persuade the writer to support them – for example with all the talk about how classless hunting is?

Look at the way the hunt monitors are presented. Do they seem reasonable people, or are they presented as fanatics?

Look at the writer's last paragraph in the main article. Does this show she is neutral, or is it poking fun at the hunters? Look at the last paragraph of the second section: what impression does the quotation here give of the hunt monitors?

Reading

🅱 Eyewitness account

In the 1920s George Orwell worked as a police officer in Burma, a country near India. One day he was expected to kill an elephant which was running wild. As you read his account, look at:

- what impression it gives you of the writer
- what you can work out about the writer's opinion of what happens.

George Orwell

❧ Shooting an elephant

BUT I DID NOT WANT TO SHOOT THE ELEPHANT. I watched him beating his bunch of grass against his knees, with that preoccupied grandmotherly air that elephants have. It seemed to me that it would be murder to shoot him. At that age I was not squeamish about killing animals, but I had never shot an elephant and never wanted to. (Somehow it always seems worse to kill a *large* animal.) Besides, there was the beast's owner to be considered. Alive, the elephant was worth at least a hundred pounds; dead, he would only be worth the value of his tusks, five pounds, possibly. But I had got to act quickly. I turned to some experienced-looking Burmans who had been there when we arrived, and asked them how the elephant had been behaving. They all said the same thing: he took no notice of you if you left him alone, but he might charge if you went too close to him.

It was perfectly clear to me what I ought to do. I ought to walk up to within, say, twenty-five yards of the elephant and test his behaviour. If he charged I could shoot, if he took no notice of me it would be safe to leave him until the mahout came back. But also I knew that I was going to do no such thing. I was a poor shot with a rifle and the ground was soft mud into which one would sink at every step. If the elephant charged and I missed him, I should have about as much chance as a toad under a steam-roller. But even then I was not thinking particularly of my own skin, only of the watchful yellow faces behind. For at that moment, with the crowd watching me, I was not afraid in the ordinary sense, as I would have been if I had been alone. A white man mustn't be frightened in front of 'natives'; and so, in general, he isn't frightened. The sole thought in my mind was that if anything went wrong those two thousand Burmans would see me pursued, caught, trampled on and reduced to a grinning corpse like that Indian up the hill. And if that happened it was quite probable that some of them would laugh. That would never do. There was only one alternative. I shoved the cartridges into the magazine and lay down on the road to get a better aim.

The crowd grew very still, and a deep, low, happy sigh, as of people who see the theatre curtain go up at last, breathed from innumerable throats. They were going to have their bit of fun after all. The rifle was a beautiful German thing with cross-hair sights. I did not then know that in shooting an elephant one would shoot to cut an imaginary bar running from ear-hole to ear-hole. I ought, therefore, as the elephant was sideways on, to have aimed straight at his ear-hole; actually I aimed several inches in front of this, thinking the brain would be further forward.

Shooting an elephant

When I pulled the trigger I did not hear the bang or feel the kick – one never does when a shot goes home – but I heard the devilish roar of glee that went up from the crowd. In that instant, in too short a time one would have thought, even for the bullet to get there, a mysterious, terrible change had come over the elephant. He neither stirred nor fell, but every line of his body had altered. He looked suddenly stricken, shrunken, immensely old, as though the frightful impact of the bullet had paralysed him without knocking him down. At last, after what seemed a long time – it might have been five seconds, I dare say – he sagged flabbily to his knees. His mouth slobbered. An enormous senility seemed to have settled upon him. One could have imagined him thousands of years old. I fired again into the same spot. At the second shot he did not collapse but climbed with desperate slowness to his feet and stood weakly upright, with legs sagging and head drooping. I fired a third time. That was the shot that did for him. You could see the agony of it jolt his whole body and knock the last remnant of strength from his legs. But in falling he seemed for a moment to rise, for as his hind legs collapsed beneath him he seemed to tower upwards like a huge rock toppling, his trunk reaching skywards like a tree. He trumpeted, for the first and only time. And then down he came, his belly towards me, with a crash that seemed to shake the ground even where I lay.

I got up. The Burmans were already racing past me across the mud. It was obvious that the elephant would never rise again, but he was not dead. He was breathing very rhythmically with long rattling gasps, his great mound of a side painfully rising and falling. His mouth was wide open – I could see far down into caverns of pale pink throat. I waited a long time for him to die, but his breathing did not weaken. Finally I fired my two remaining shots into the spot where I thought his heart must be. The thick blood welled out of him like red velvet, but still he did not die. His body did not even jerk when the shots hit him, the tortured breathing continued without a pause. He was dying, very slowly and in great agony, but in some world remote from me where not even a bullet could damage him further. I felt that I had got to put an end to that dreadful noise. It seemed dreadful to see the great beast lying there, powerless to move and yet powerless to die, and not even to be able to finish him. I sent back for my small rifle and poured shot after shot into his heart and down his throat. They seemed to make no impression. The tortured gasps continued as steadily as the ticking of a clock.

In the end I could not stand it any longer and went away. I heard later that it took him half an hour to die. Burmans were bringing dahs and baskets even before I left, and I was told they had stripped his body almost to the bones by the afternoon.

GEORGE ORWELL

Word bank

dah   short heavy sword, used as a knife
mahout   elephant keeper
remnant   remains
senility   a confused mental state that can come with old age

A

1   Give one reason why George Orwell does not want to kill the elephant.   (2 marks)

2   George Orwell is worried about what the Burmese spectators might think of him. What is he afraid of?   (2 marks)

3   Why does Orwell not stay to watch the death of the elephant?   (2 marks)

B

4   Many readers are disturbed by George Orwell's attitude to the Burmese people around him. Write a paragraph about the way he describes them, and his attitude to them.

(6 marks)

Advice   Look at the way he describes the crowd – labelling them by their colour – and the words he uses to describe the differences between them and himself. Notice the pressure he feels to do the right thing – what is his main concern here? Look at the way the crowd react to the shooting of the elephant – the words Orwell uses to describe the sounds they make. Do you find anything disturbing about Orwell's attitude? Explain why/why not.

5   How does George Orwell use language to help the reader to visualize the death of the elephant? What feelings do you think he expects us to have?   (8 marks)

Advice   Notice that before he kills the elephant he thinks about the process. If he got it wrong he would be like 'a toad under a steam-roller'. Why does he give us a long build-up before showing us how he pulled the trigger? Notice how the reaction of the elephant is described step-by-step. Is the description visual – do the words help you to see exactly what happened? Which words are most powerful? Look out for similes ('blood… like red velvet') and describe their effect. Does Orwell describe all of this neutrally, without emotion? Look out for images of the elephant's suffering and the use of words like 'dreadful'. What effect do these have in shaping our response to the text?

Writing to argue, persuade or instruct

A Newspaper report

Imagine that you are someone with strong views on fox-hunting. You feel it is a cruel and unnecessary sport. You have just read Lynne Wallis's article and it has made you angry. You feel that she does not show how much the foxes suffer; she treats the subject as something of a joke; and she seems more interested in the backgrounds of the people than in the real issue of hunting.

Write a letter of complaint to the Editor of the *Daily Express*. Say what you feel is wrong with the article and how you think it could have been improved. Keep your tone formal rather than chatty.

Advice For advice on writing letters see Self-Help Sheets 4 and 5 in the Answer Book.

B Eyewitness account

Elephants are still being unlawfully killed by poachers in Africa and India. Using George Orwell's account as your starting-point, put together a leaflet aimed at gaining support from readers to outlaw all hunting. The aim of your leaflet should be to get people to sign a petition saying that any killing of elephants is wrong.

Write a persuasive leaflet, perhaps using some of George Orwell's account of how the elephant suffers before it dies. Use layout to make your leaflet visually striking.

Advice Look at the examples of leaflets on pages 12–26.
For practical advice on creating a leaflet, see Self-Help Sheet 1 in the Answer Book.

Reportage comparison 1

Introduction

Read the two texts on pages 29-31 and 33-34. Both describe accounts of hunting. Text A is a newspaper report from the *Daily Express*; text B is George Orwell's personal account of shooting an elephant.

Comparison

Reporting styles
Use the questions below to compare the texts.

A

1 'The hunters in the first text are looking forward to the hunt.'

'George Orwell hates the idea of killing the elephant.'

Find a quotation from each text which supports these statements. (2 marks)

2 Write down one clue that the first text is a piece of journalism. (2 marks)

3 Write down one clue that George Orwell's text is personal. (2 marks)

B

4 What differences do you notice in the way the two texts are written? You might comment upon:

- which is easier to follow
- which is more emotional
- what we learn about the writer from each text
- how their use of language differs. (14 marks)

Reportage comparison 2

Introduction This unit looks more closely at newspaper styles. Newspapers are probably the form of reportage we know best – after all, they are usually written by 'reporters'. In Britain people usually talk about two types of newspapers: the tabloid and the broadsheet.

Tabloid	Broadsheet
for example: the *Sun*, the *Mirror*, the *Express*, the *Mail*	for example: the *Times*, the *Independent*, the *Daily Telegraph*
smaller format – more convenient to read – lots of images and eye-catching headlines	larger format, and generally more text
snappy, fast-moving style, lots of labels ('Top actor Rick Ratcliff, 27…')	usually a more formal style – still aiming to entertain as well as inform the reader, but in a more restrained way
lots of emphasis on showbusiness, royalty, gossip	more emphasis on politics and hard news

Remember also that any newspaper will contain a range of writing for different purposes – some reporting news, some 'features writing' looking at other issues which may not be directly topical. There will be sports writing, reviews, perhaps problem pages – a huge range of writing styles.

The best way to tune into the differences in approach and style of the two types of newspaper is to compare them. In this unit, look at how the *Express* and the *Daily Telegraph* report the same story.

Skills checklist **Reading newspaper articles**
- Understand what the newspaper story is about.
- Comment on the way the story is written.
- Make judgements about whether the writer seems to be objective (neutral) or biased.

Writing newspaper articles
- Your headline needs to capture the reader's attention.
- Your first paragraph should summarize the whole story – who, what, where and when?

- Your story should usually include quotes from experts or eyewitnesses – to give the article a more factual feel.

Language features To gain higher grades at GCSE you'll need to be able to discuss the language of newspaper articles. Look out for:

- attention-grabbing headlines – usually shorter than eight words long
- headlines which compress as much information as possible into a short space. To add drama they usually use the present rather than the past tense. They often leave out auxiliary verbs (like 'was', 'were', 'have'): 'Plane Crashes' rather than 'A Plane Has Crashed'
- short paragraphs to keep the story fast-moving (in most newspapers – but not all)
- dramatic words like 'drama', 'crisis', 'bid', 'crash' – used particularly in tabloid journalism
- sentences which are usually straightforward and not too long.

Advice panel

- Practise comparing the same news story in different papers – begin to get a better feel for the differences between tabloid and broadsheet journalism.
- When responding to newspaper articles, remember to comment as closely as you can on the use of language – for example, the compressed language of the headline; the summarizing first sentence; the vocabulary; the short paragraphs.
- You might also comment on the use of photographs to illustrate the story. What image is shown? What impression does it add to the story? What size is the photo and what might this tell us about the story's importance?
- When writing a newspaper article, keep the pace of your article fast. Choose words which won't slow the reader down because she has to look them up – at the same time, they should be precise, well-chosen words. Remember that much journalism is written against quite tight deadlines: make yourself practise the same.
- Most journalism is trying to inform and entertain. Make sure your article doesn't just recite the facts but presents them in an attention-grabbing way.

Comparison

Tabloid and broadsheet journalism

These two newspaper articles tell the same story – of a dramatic rescue in Anglesey, North Wales. Compare the way the story is treated in the *Express* (page 40) and the *Daily Telegraph* (page 41). Look out in particular for differences in:

- language
- the facts that are given
- the order in which information is presented.

Text A

Helicopter dash saves dive twins

BY TONY BROOKS

AN RAF helicopter crew 'wave hopped' for 70 miles yesterday to protect two divers feared to be suffering from the bends.

Twins Ian and Stuart Middle, 27, had tried in vain to save another diver who got into trouble in a disused quarry. They brought him to the surface quickly, risking the bends.

The Sea King helicopter took the twins from the quarry near Talysarn in Snowdonia to the nearest decompression chamber at Murrayfield Hospital in the Wirral.

Throughout the trip the helicopter rarely flew higher than 30ft, swooping under power lines and the Britannia and Menai bridges, which link Anglesey to the mainland, before continuing just above the Irish Sea, hugging the North Wales coast. Pilot, Flight Lieutenant Steve Hayward, from RAF Valley, Anglesey, said: 'To have flown above the bridges and power lines would have meant going to 500ft and this could have had a serious effect on the two divers.

'It is always vital to fly as low as possible when taking divers for treatment.'

'We skimmed waves and flew under bridges'

The twins spent two and a quarter hours in the hospital's chamber before being moved to a ward where they spent the night under observation. A spokesman said: 'Both men are stable and we do not anticipate any problems. They should be released within 24 hours.

'They have been very fortunate. In circumstances like these they could have been paralysed or suffered a stroke.' The bends are caused by a sudden change in pressure as a diver comes to the surface. Nitrogen gets into body tissues forming bubbles which can affect the joints, bloodstream, spine and brain.

Ian and Stuart are members of the Warwickshire Sub-Aqua Club. The dead diver, who comes from Coventry, was not a member of their group. Last night he had not been officially identified.

The quarry has a reputation as a danger spot, and there have been calls for it to be closed because of the number of incidents involving divers who get into trouble and the cost of flying them out for treatment.

Last month an inquest on a 29-year-old bank manager who died at a depth of more than 100ft heard how ice capsules can form in breathing equipment.

The Daily Express,
10 November 1997

Pilot flies below bridges to save divers

By Barbie Dutter

AN RAF helicopter carrying two divers with 'the bends' made a dramatic rescue flight beneath two bridges and a power cable yesterday to avoid potentially lethal pressure changes.

Ian and Stuart Middle, 27-year-old twin brothers, had risen too quickly to the surface of a quarry pool while attempting to rescue a fellow diver in Snowdonia.

The pair had been diving at depths of more than 150ft at the disused Dorothea slate quarry near Caernarfon when they found their stricken colleague.

They brought the man to the surface in less than two minutes, but attempts by paramedics to revive him failed. He is thought to have run out of air and drowned.

The brothers were picked up by a Sea King helicopter from RAF Valley in Anglesey for an 80-mile flight to the Murrayfield Hospital, Thingwall, Wirral, which has a recompression chamber.

When divers rise too quickly, nitrogen bubbles can form in the bloodstream, tissues or joints, causing decompression illness – known as the bends.

The helicopter crew, aware that changes in pressure could precipitate or exacerbate the condition, decided to

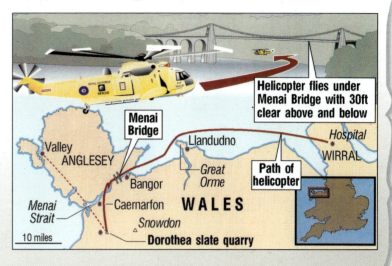

fly the aircraft as close to sea level as possible.

The 40-minute flight involved flying under power lines across the Menai Strait and beneath the Britannia and Menai bridges linking Anglesey with the mainland. As the helicopter flew beneath the bridges, there was only 30ft to spare above and below it.

The pilot, Flt Lt Steve Hayward, said yesterday: 'To have flown above the bridges and power lines would have meant going to 500ft, and this could have had an effect on the pressure.'

Another member of the four-strong rescue crew, Sgt Rich Taylor, added: 'The brothers were obviously quite shocked, although they did very well, putting themselves at risk to bring the other guy up.'

He insisted that yesterday's

rescue flight had been routine. 'It's really quite common for search and rescue helicopters to carry "bendy" divers, and it is standard flying procedure to stay as low as possible. We had more than ample room to go under the bridges and power lines, and we took our time.'

The two brothers, from Warwickshire, spent more than two hours in the recompression chamber as a precautionary measure and were kept in hospital overnight.

Dr John Harrison, director of the hospital's hyperbaric unit, said decompression illness usually developed within 12 to 24 hours.

'The two men are in fairly good spirits, all things considered,' he said.

The Daily Telegraph,
10 November 1997

A

1 Say, in a sentence, what happened to Ian and Stuart Middle.

(2 marks)

2 Why did the pilot decide to fly under the Menai bridge?

(2 marks)

B

3 Look at the headlines for each story. Which one do you think works best? Write a short paragraph saying why.

(4 marks)

Advice

Which is more dramatic? Look at the use of 'dash' and 'dive twins' in the *Express*.

Which gives you more information? Which makes you want to read on?

4 Look at the first paragraph of each version. Write about the differences you notice.

(4 marks)

Advice

You might comment on:
- which gives the better summary of the story
- which contains more detail
- use of the phrase 'wave hopped' in the *Express*

- the vocabulary of the *Daily Telegraph* – for example, 'potentially lethal' – and what this shows about the audience.

5 How helpful do you find the map in the *Telegraph*? (2 marks)

6 What features of language in both texts do you find typical of newspaper writing? What differences do you notice?

(6 marks)

Advice   Look again at the headlines – note the tense used.

Look at the first paragraph – how do the writers in each case tell the full story? Why don't they give more detailed information in the first paragraph – like the name of the pilot?

Look at the vocabulary, especially in the *Express* – 'dash', 'feared'.

Look for ways in which people are labelled.

Look at the way quotations are used. Look at the way background information is added – e.g. details about the quarry and an earlier incident.

Which text feels more factual and more detailed? How can you tell? In your last sentence try to summarize the main differences you notice in the two articles.

Writing to argue, persuade or instruct

Imagine you are Ian or Stuart Middle and you are writing a diary account of what happened to you and your brother. Which were the worst and best moments? How did you feel at different times?

Write your diary entry, trying to describe what happened and how you felt.

Use today's date as your starting-point.

Advice   For practical advice on writing a diary entry, see Self-Help Sheet 9 in the Answer Book.

Autobiography

Autobiography is someone's writing about her- or himself. When we read these texts, we expect to learn about the person involved – perhaps a celebrity, or someone famous in history, or someone we admire – and to find out about the pattern of their lives. At its worst, autobiography can read like a list: 'I did this... then I did that.' But the best autobiography does more than tell us what happened; it shows us how and why certain events took place, and the writer might reflect on how she or he has changed as a result.

Autobiographies come in as many different styles as novels. Some have an informal, chatty style – and work hard to capture and hold our attention:

> I would have recognized that backside anywhere. It loomed large above the surprisingly slim ankles, waited impatiently as the arms transferred parcels, one to the other, and then it swivelled and slammed into the glass doors before charging triumphantly backwards in Marks and Spencer, dragging my mother along in its wake...
>
> *Deric Longden,* LOST FOR WORDS

Here the writer uses a saucy opening sentence to hook us, then keeps us guessing about who is being described.

Other writers are writing about their own experiences in a more literary style:

> We are going by car from Bulaq Dakhur to Heliopolis. I am in the back. The leather of the seat sticks to my bare legs. We travel along a road lined at either side with oleander and jacaranda trees, alternate splashes of white and blue...
>
> *Penelope Lively,* A CHILDHOOD PERCEIVED

Notice how the writer creates a sense of atmosphere – inside the car and out. Notice also how she uses the present tense – 'I am...' rather than 'I was...'. The effect is to make the events she describes feel immediate – happening now, as if she is reliving them before our eyes.

Skills checklist

Reading autobiography

- As you read, try to build up a picture of the person whose life is at the centre of the writing.
- Absorb clues about the social and historical context – what life was like around the person.
- Notice how structure helps to create an effect: some writers tell their story from start to finish; others break the story up, moving backwards and forwards in time.

Writing autobiography

- Bring personal experiences to life for an audience who may not know you.
- Make your account lively and vivid.
- Write in a style which goes beyond just listing events.

Language features

To gain higher grades at GCSE you'll need to be able to discuss the language of autobiography. Look out for:

- how much the writer uses the first person mode ('I...')
- ways in which the writer manages to avoid using 'I' all the time
- the use of words to create a powerful atmosphere
- parts of the text in which the writer changes mode: instead of just describing what has happened to her, she instead reflects on the impact of certain events
- techniques the writer uses to hold our interest – for example, telling her life-story in a different order, building suspense, holding back some information to keep us guessing, using dialogue to show the words people actually say.

Advice panel

- Read some autobiographies. Try to become familiar with a range of different styles – the brisk, factual styles in some sporting autobiographies; the more technical style of politicians' memoirs; the lively, unpredictable approach in autobiographies by rock stars.
- Compare the opening paragraphs of some different autobiographies – look at how writers try to grab their readers' attention.
- Remember the three main areas of interest in studying autobiographies: what the writer is like; what the background context is like; and how the text is written.

A **'My Mam's Death'**

This text was written by teenager Samantha Studley, as she thinks back to a terrible time in her own life. As you read, think about:

- what impression you get of the writer
- who the text is aimed at.

❧ MY MAM'S DEATH ❧

WHEN I WAS FOURTEEN AND A HALF YEARS OLD, my Mother (who was aged forty-two) died of cancer. At first, before she started to get really ill in December '82, my Dad had to get the doctor out to her. When the doctor came out and he said that she would have to go into hospital for an operation on ulcers in her stomach, or so I thought anyway. She had the operation on 6 January 1983, and it turned out that she had cancer of the bowel. The doctor told my Dad that she would live for another year at the most.

She came through the operation quite well, which really built up my hopes that she'd pull through, because at the time I didn't know that she never had long to live. About two weeks after the operation, she got a bit better, talking, reading and just able to walk about a little bit. She came out of hospital in mid-February, and came home for a few weeks to stay with her Mother (my Gran) for rest and peace.

My dad and my older brothers and sisters knew from the start she was dying, after the operation. Then just before she came back home to stay with us, my Dad gave me the shattering news about my Mam: 'I know I should have told you this a long time ago but your Mam's dying.' Just like that. I ran upstairs to my bedroom, and I broke down in tears. If he'd told me from the start, then I wouldn't have taken it so bad as I did. The few days after that, before Mam came out of hospital, were sheer hell, I just couldn't accept that my mother was going to die, no way. She can't just leave me like that, after fourteen years with her as her daughter.

I couldn't wait for Mam to come home. I cleaned up the house from top to bottom, did the washing, ironing and made the beds so that the place would look spotless for her homecoming. I got flowers for her bedroom and the living room.

She came home just after Easter in 1983, and she was all right the first few days after coming home. I had to stay away (with special permission) from school to look after her, and my two-year-old brother Gerard (now four), while Dad went shopping.

In early May she gradually just got worse everyday. She couldn't eat and had to stay in bed, wearing a colostomy bag. All day and night she couldn't sleep and she kept taking tablets and pills all the time. I could hear her crying in the nights, which was the first time I'd ever heard her cry, and it used to break my heart. She lost loads of weight, and she couldn't walk. She was as thin as a matchstick and weighed about four stone. I used to look at her sitting in the chair like a vegetable, and she had to be carried everywhere. She couldn't go out anywhere, and because we had just got a new house, which should've been for Mam, she wanted to go and see it which was absolutely impossible for her because of her condition. Then in the early morning, about five a.m. on 2 June, she fell into a deep coma and after some final words she died at eight-thirty a.m. My life just fell apart. My Dad was a widower and my two-year-old brother was left (and me) to grow up without a mother.

After the death I just sat and moped about the house, lost weight, never ate much and I lost sleep. I stayed in every night for about a month, lost contact with all my friends, until my Dad encouraged me to go out again and face the world. I went to school the following week and gradually I picked up the shattered pieces of my torn apart life. My Mam was devoted to us, and she wanted my Dad to take great care of us.

She still remains in my life, because I'm part of her, and I shed a tear now and again for her.

Samantha Studley

Word bank   **colostomy bag**   a plastic sack attached to the patient's body into which the waste fluids flow

A

1 What ages were the narrator and her younger brother when their mother died? (2 marks)

2 How does the narrator think her father should have handled the news that her mother was dying? (4 marks)

B

3 Why do you think the narrator spends so long getting the house ready for her mother's return from hospital? (4 marks)

Advice Think about how she wants her mum to feel. Think also of the impression she is trying to create of her own role.

4 The writer doesn't include any words spoken by the mother – we hear about her, but we don't hear from her. Why do you think this is? (5 marks)

Advice Would the presence of the mother in the text make a big difference? Would it change the balance or focus of the text, shifting the emphasis onto biography rather than autobiography? Would it make it a more emotional text? Do you think the narrator has avoided quoting her mother because this may be too personal?

5 Write a paragraph about your response to the text. Do you find it emotional, moving, controlled, neutral? What do you notice about the way the writer has written it? (5 marks)

Advice Don't assume that the text keeps the same style throughout – look for parts which are catalogues of what happened. How are they written? Then find the other parts which are more reflective – someone thinking back over the effect an experience has upon her. Look at the vocabulary – is it formal or informal? Is the tone chatty or factual? How does the emotional content work for you? Is it controlled, or is there too much emotion? Remember to support your response with quotations.

Reading   **B** **'Cursed'**

The following text was written in the 1930s by David Swift, born with a muscle disease. For him, his chief challenge is not the disability; it is the attitude of his parents. As you read, think about:

● what impression you get of the writer
● who the text is aimed at.

⋙ Cursed ⋘

MY GRANDMA USED TO SAY that I'd been cursed and that I was being punished by God for what I'd done in a past life. That was why I was disabled she said, and when I'd served out this punishment everything would be all right. I used to wonder what it was I'd done so bad to make me like this. I felt as if, well, if I'm cursed I ought to be aware of why, didn't I? But I had no idea what it could be. Nobody seemed to care. Perhaps my mum and dad were trying to cope with their own lives, I don't know. But they never showed me any affection. I couldn't speak about my feelings because weakness wasn't tolerated. My dad made me hard, hard inside. He was always wanting me to be tough. He never showed me any sympathy and I never felt like there was any love for me there. I felt as though I were different, like a freak in a side show. I remember when we all used to go to Nottingham Goose Fair and they used to have side shows and all the freaks would lay there. And I always remember thinking to myself. I wonder if I should sit up there with my feet showing? You know and people pay sixpence a time, coming in and looking at my feet. There was nobody else around like me was there? There was nowhere else I could go. I used to have this great fear that they would get rid of me or put me down because I was disabled. Fathers used to take cats and drown them in the river and I used to think that's the way they would do it to me, that's the way they killed you. We had a dog called Pete and he broke his leg. So they decided to have him destroyed and I used to think, well, why destroy dogs that can walk on three legs? I thought, perhaps they put human beings down as well, perhaps they'll destroy me, because I can't walk? I used to spend a lot of time on my own in the graveyard. I used to ponder over all the things that you saw on the grave-stones you know. I used to think, I wonder if God needs me more than they, I wonder if God's wanting me? I didn't want God to want me, I was too young. I wanted to stay on this earth. I had this constant fear that they were going to get me. I didn't want to die.

David Swift

A

1   How does David Swift's grandmother explain his
     disability?   (2 marks)

2   Find a sentence which shows that David Swift blamed
     himself for being disabled.   (2 marks)

3   What point is the writer making when he talks about cats
     and dogs?   (2 marks)

B

4   Look at the influence on David Swift of his family – in
     particular his grandmother, mother and father. What effect
     do their words have upon him?   (6 marks)

Advice   Does he blame his parents? Do you think his grandmother was actually
              trying to make him feel better?

5   Write a paragraph about your impressions of David Swift's
     character, supporting your points with close reference to
     the language of the extract.   (8 marks)

Advice   Look at how he feels after visiting
              Nottingham Goose Fair, and the
              effect on him of the way dogs are
              treated.
              What do we learn from his time
              alone in graveyards?
              What point is he making at the end
              about God, and what does this
              show about his character?
              Look at the written style. Does it feel
              like a formal, written text, or is there
              a more conversational tone?
              Support your ideas with examples.
              Who do you think he is addressing?
              (For example, is he writing the text
              for himself or for others?) How can
              you tell?
              Why do you think he is writing the
              text – to tell others about his
              experiences, or to try to come to
              terms with his own feelings? Again,
              support your ideas with examples.

Writing to argue, persuade or instruct

A My Mam's Death

Write a profile of Samantha Studley for her local newspaper.
In it, try to show not only what she has gone through, but
also the kind of person she is – her courage, organization, and
positive outlook, for example. Your profile should give
readers a clear picture of who she is. You might use the
headline: 'Local Hero at Fourteen-and-a-half'.

Advice   To look at examples of biography – people writing about other people – see pages 71–81.

For practical advice on writing a newspaper profile, see Self-Help Sheets 2 and 3 in the Answer Book.

 Cursed

Imagine that someone in David Swift's family – such as his grandmother or father – reads his account of growing up and feeling 'cursed'. Imagine their feelings of guilt at the way they spoke and behaved. Write a letter from one of them to David explaining what they did and apologizing.

Start:

Dear David,

I have just read your account of being 'cursed from birth...

Advice   To look at examples of letters see pages 109–118.
For practical advice on writing a letter, see Self-Help Sheets 4 and 5 in the Answer Book.

Travel writing

Travel writing is a genre which has gained in popularity in the past fifteen years or so. It is probably closest in style to autobiography. We usually follow one person's account of places they have been and people they have seen.

The writer's purpose might vary. Some travel writers, especially those writing in newspapers, are telling us about a place which readers might themselves choose to visit. Their purpose is similar to the film or theatre critic who reviews a movie or play to tell us whether it is worth seeing. Their style is likely to be quite factual, with a feeling that they are addressing readers with a clear purpose in mind:

> Sometimes, particularly if you are feeling threatened or insecure, it is difficult to tell whether people are being genuine or 'hustling'. But if you are cautious and rely on your instincts, then you might find, as I did, that Moroccans are incredibly hospitable people, many of whom love to have Westerners to stay...
>
> *Pat Chell*, THREE KINDS OF WOMAN

Notice the style here: Pat Chell tells us what she notices, but it doesn't feel like pure autobiography. She clearly has a wish to instruct the reader – to tell us what we should know about Morocco based upon her experiences.

Compare that 'didactic' style of writing (*didactic* means to teach) with this:

About four o'clock we struck some more plantations, and passing through these, came to a path running north-east, down which we went. I must say the forest scenery here was superbly lovely. Along this mountain side cliff to the mangrove swamp the sun could reach the soil, owing to the steepness and abruptness and the changes of curves off the ground; while the soft steamy air which came up off the swamp swathed everything, and although unpleasantly strong in smell to us, was yet evidently highly agreeable to the vegetation.

Mary Kingsley, TRAVELS IN WEST AFRICA

Notice the different style here – the emphasis on descriptive writing (with adjectives like 'lovely', 'soft', 'steamy' and adverbs like 'unpleasantly', 'highly', 'superbly'); the sense of fascination at what she is seeing; and the overall aim of recreating in language what has been experienced.

These are just two examples of travel writing. The range of styles is huge. As you read, keep thinking about the writer's audience and purpose.

Skills checklist

Reading travel writing
- Understand the text.
- Comment on what we learn about the people and places described.
- Make judgements about the character of the narrator.
- Comment on the writer's use of language.

Writing travel writing
- Give a powerful sense of people and places.
- Use language descriptively and precisely (not just strings of adjectives and adverbs).
- Use language to reflect upon why a place is important to you – the effect it has had upon you.

Language features

To gain higher grades, you need to be able to show you are aware of the language features of travel writing. Look out for:

- a style of writing which might resemble autobiography, with strong emphasis on the thoughts and feelings of the writer
- descriptive language to create a powerful sense of people and places
- events described as part of a narrative – placed in the order that they took place
- in some forms of travel writing, a more didactic tone – giving advice to the reader about the suitability of certain places.

Advice panel • • • • • • • • • • • • • • • • • • •

- Try to read a range of travel writing – for example, in weekend newspapers (many have travel sections), and in anthologies of travel writing: M Morris and L O'Connor, *The Virago Book of Women Travellers*, Jonathan Raban, *The Oxford Book of the Sea*, Geoff Barton, *Travel Writing*.
- Look closely at the text – what do you learn about the writer? How is she using language to communicate her observations and ideas?
- Keep your own journal of observations and descriptions – even if it's only of your journey to school. It will help you to sharpen your own descriptive writing.

Reading

A Hitching through the Yukon

Kate Pullinger is a Canadian writer who lives in London. Here she describes the experience of hitch-hiking through the Yukon region of Western Canada. As you read, think about:

- what the author's main message is
- who it is aimed at.

Hitching through the Yukon

THE YUKON is basically the 'Great Outdoors', and not much else. Exceptionally underpopulated, with less than 25,000 people in an area almost as large as France, it is a mountain-lake-forest-river-lover's dream come true. I think the best way to see it, at least in summer, is to hitch-hike. I have always found hitching in the Yukon relatively fast, easy and safe, mainly because towns are far apart and nobody is going to leave anyone standing on the side of the road in the middle of nowhere at -20° C, or, in summer, in all that dust.

Last summer I stood on the side of the road outside the Yukon's capital, Whitehorse. My thumb stuck out, I was heading for Dawson City 333 miles away. The first vehicle to stop was an old Ford truck, bed on back with two extremely large sled dogs hanging out over its sides. They barked at me ferociously. A woman jumped out and asked how far I was going. I told her, and she said she was only going fifty miles, but that was a good start. So I jumped in.

She was young, had long plaited hair, and was wearing men's shorts and a felt hat. Next to her sat a small, dark baby, who looked at me curiously. The woman didn't say anything so neither did I. After a few miles she reached above the windscreen and pulled a cigar from behind the sunshade. She smoked it as she drove, clenching it between her teeth when she changed gear. I looked out of the window over the hills and vast, peopleless landscape.

After fifty miles she pulled off the road on to the dirt track that led to her house and I thanked her and jumped out. I slammed the truck door so it shut properly and she and the baby sped off. The sled dogs barked at me until I was far out of their sight.

I stood again at the side of the road. A small Toyota two-door stopped. I put my pack in the back seat and climbed in front. This driver was also a woman, she wore a skirt and her hair was wet. We began to chat and I learned that she was just driving home from a swimming lesson in Whitehorse – a trip of 200 miles, which she made every Friday. There aren't very many swimming pools in the Yukon. The conversation led to a familiar story: she came up to the Yukon ten years ago to visit a friend and stayed. She said she wouldn't leave for anything, and now her brother lives up here too. I began to think there must be something special about this place.

Where she dropped me it was very quiet. There were trees everywhere I looked. In fact, all I could see was trees. I had to wait here around twenty minutes before I heard what sounded like a truck. I saw the dust before I could see it, great clouds of dirt billowing up into the sky. Then I saw the truck and stood on my tiptoes and tried to make my thumb bigger. The driver saw me and started to slow down. It took him a long time to do so and he went past me. I could no longer see, there was so much dust, and I held my scarf over my mouth. When it settled I walked to the truck – a long way up – and negotiated the lift, another fifty miles.

After hoisting my pack up I climbed in. The driver started the engine and headed down the road. I smiled to myself, thinking I was in front of the dust now. The truck driver seemed to change gears a hundred times before we were up to the right speed.

Steaming along, past the endless lakes and hills, he told me about his children going to school, having babies and working in Edmonton. I listened and then asked how long he'd been here. He said he came for a year thirty years ago. There is something about this place.

KATE PULLINGER

A

1 How large is the Yukon territory and what is its population?

(2 marks)

2 In the extract, Kate Pullinger meets three different drivers. Write a sentence about each describing who they are.

(6 marks)

B

3 At the end of the extract, Kate Pullinger says, 'There is something about this place'. What do you think she means?

(4 marks)

4 What do we learn about the Yukon from the extract?

(4 marks)

Advice

Look again at the first two paragraphs – they contain some factual details about the environment.
Look also at the distances of the place – and the way people respond to them (for example, the woman driving the Toyota).
Look at the third and last-but-one paragraphs, which describe some of the features of the landscape.

5 What impression do you gain of Kate Pullinger from the extract?

(4 marks)

Advice

Look at the beginning and the way she describes hitch-hiking. What clues do her comments give you about her personality?
Look at the way she reacts to some of the people who give her rides.
Does she seem tolerant, friendly? Does she judge or criticize them? Look at the way she responds to the landscape – any clues here about her outlook? Does she seem adventurous?

Reading

B **Travelling through the Sahara**

In 1982 Michael Asher went to live with the Kababish tribe who roam the drought-stricken Sahara desert. Here, he is travelling with a group of nomads when suddenly a vicious storm blows up. As you read, think about:

● what the author's main message is
● who it is aimed at.

A DESERT DIES

AFTER DARK a savage sand-storm punched into us with hammer force. We made camp at once by a single bush, a tiny island in the void. As we piled up our equipment, the wind screamed past us, pouring liquid sand into everything. The storm was as thick as a blizzard. It was a struggle to cook up our *kisri*, to build up a fortress of saddle-bags around the fire, which flickered and trembled in the wind. The porridge was covered with sand as soon as we tried to eat it. After we had eaten what we could, we had no alternative but to disappear under our blankets. Sand piled up into drifts around us, and as the night grew colder and the wind more icy, we shivered at the base of our lone bush.

In the morning we were half buried in a drift of sand. The wind was still so bitterly cold that we huddled close to the fire, wrapped up tightly, until the sun came up. We watched its pale glow turning the desert luminescent, the horizons fuzzy and insubstantial. The flat plain, embossed with the shining lumps of low dunes, was licked by slip-streams of sand that streaked across the surface like currents of electricity.

We drove the herd out into the eye of the wind, all of us walking in the shelter of the great animal bodies. The wind showed no sign of dropping and all day the storm raged over us, white-out on all sides. The camels were reluctant to travel into the squall and we had to force them on with our whips.

Often we came upon tall clumps of *nissa* grass and tangled masses of *tundub* trees, and the hungry camels broke formation to graze, disappearing into the veil of dust. When this happened it took many minutes to reassemble them. The entire day we moved in short bursts with little progress. 'We are going badly!' Musa Adam shouted at me through his furled headcloth. 'At this rate it will be another twenty-six days to

Isna. I don't know what the guide is doing. We keep turning and circling, but we should go on straight. Moving is better than grazing for these camels now!' I thought the comment unfair, and I checked the compass-bearing I had taken the previous day at Umm Grayn. It was no more than two degrees out.

At mid-morning we stopped amongst some rocks and made porridge, our faces still covered in our headcloths. As Sannat and I lay in the shelter of the rocks, he told me, 'The Arabs hate sand-storms more than anything. How many people have lost their way in them and died! Even experienced desert-men can die in a storm like this. Don't listen to anyone who tells you anything different. There is no Arab alive who can navigate in these storms unless he has travelled the route scores of times. Only last year a guide was taking a *dabuuka* past Jabal al 'Ain when he ran out of water in a storm like this. He tried to make for the spring in Al 'Ain but he lost the way and all his men died. It is a good thing old Bakheit and I know the way!'

That afternoon the desert was at its wildest. We lapped ourselves around with blankets and headcloths and bent forward into the wind as we walked, plodding on in the soft sand. We wound through great fields of boulders that channelled the streams of dust into flying eddies, and after them came more patches of sand, red and amber, hard dunes littered with basalt, and a narrow pass that was converted by the dust into a long tunnel with neither entrance nor exit.

The storm went on for three days. It was a grim time, yet solid old Bakheit never wavered. He was a silent man, not given to bursts of excitement as most Arabs were. He rarely walked like the rest of us, but rode his gigantic camel on and on, unperturbed by the wind or the sand, the cold or the heat, never irritated by the nagging stoppages nor the criticisms of the others. He and Sannat belonged to a different breed from the Sarajab I had travelled with. They were certainly of slave stock, yet they were huge, massively powerful men who seemed to be hewn from the granite of the desert itself.

On the evening of the third day the storm dropped suddenly. The sky cleared, and the golden beams of the dwindling sun spread out across it like the arms of a giant starfish. The sea-spray hiss of the wind stopped abruptly; there was silence. Far to the north we saw the solid sandstone citadel of Jabal al 'Ain springing up from the void of orange sand.

We spent a peaceful night and in the morning drove the camels across the almost featureless sand-sheet, smoothed and rolled flat by the storm. Sannat was walking on the right flank of the herd, a bulky black figure with a whip in his hand. Suddenly he stopped and shouted, 'Hey, brothers, look at this!' Several of us ran over to where he stood, and saw a broad swath of camel tracks, thousands upon thousands of them swelling over each other and spreading out thirty metres across the sand.

'It is a *dabuuka*,' he said. 'And it is not far ahead. They must have passed us in the night. Now they will be before us to market in Cairo.'

'Not if we catch them first!' Bakkour said.

Michael Asher

Word bank

basalt hard rock
dabuuka camel herd
embossed printed on, standing out from
hewn carved
kisri porridge made from millet
luminescent glowing
squall heavy wind

A

1 How long does the storm last? (2 marks)

2 Why are desert storms like this such a threat to the people of the desert? (2 marks)

3 Why, at the end of the extract, do they need to rush? (2 marks)

B

4 Michael Asher uses a number of images to create a picture in the reader's mind. Say in your own words what you understand by these images:

'a savage sand-storm punched into us with hammer force' (2 marks)

'sand that streaked across the surface like currents of electricity' (2 marks)

'disappearing into the veil of dust' (2 marks)

'the golden beams of the dwindling sun spread out... like the arms of a giant starfish' (2 marks)

5 Look more closely at the first paragraph. How does Michael Asher use language to suggest the power of the storm?

(6 marks)

Advice

Look at the words Michael Asher uses to describe the storm itself. How does he show its power and aggression?
Notice also how he describes the humans. How does he emphasize their fragility and vulnerability? Look at the description of the fire they are seated near. How does this description further suggest the storm's power?

Writing to argue, persuade or instruct

A Hitching through the Yukon

Based on Kate Pullinger's travel writing, create a magazine advertisement designed to attract more visitors to the Yukon. In it, describe the scenery, the open spaces, the friendly people and the pleasure to be enjoyed from travelling.

To create your advertisement, think of a good heading, a suitable image (just sketch it briefly), and then the text which will help to persuade your readers to send off for more information.

Advice To look at examples of advertising see pages 64–69 and 94-101.
For practical advice on writing advertisements, see Self-Help Sheet 8 in the Answer Book.

B Travelling through the Sahara

Imagine that you have been asked to simplify Michael Asher's text for a younger audience. A nature magazine aimed at 10–12 year olds wants to use it to show the danger and excitement of being in the desert; but at present the extract is too long and too difficult.

Write a simpler version of around 150 words, trying to keep all of the excitement, but making it easier for the reader to follow.

Advice For practical advice on summarizing and simplifying, see Self-Help Sheet 14 in the Answer Book.

Campaigning advertisements

Introduction

Advertising comes in many forms – posters, television, radio and cinema commercials, magazine and newspaper advertisements, and so on. At their most basic level, advertisements are saying, 'Buy this product'. Usually they will employ a number of techniques to make the product attractive – for example showing you how it will make you more successful (more healthy, more attractive, more contented, better looking) if you buy it.

This unit looks at a different form of advertising. It doesn't aim to sell a product but does try to persuade us to *do* something. Charity advertisements want us to notice the charity more, and to give either practical help or financial support.

Advertising like this needs first to catch our attention, then to touch our emotions enough to make us react. Look at two examples in this unit of how the advertisers manage it.

Skills checklist

Reading advertisements

- Understand the main points of the advertisement.
- Comment on how the language, layout, and images contribute to the effect.
- Judge how successful the advertisement is.

Writing advertisements

- Have a clear sense of your target audience.
- Use language and layout to grab their attention.
- Write a powerful persuasive text.

Language features

To gain higher grades at GCSE you'll need to be able to discuss the language of charity campaign advertisements. Look out for:

- emotional words to provoke a reaction
- specific names of people – to make the charity's work feel very personal
- stories about real-life crises, and about people who have suffered
- eye-catching layout to grab our attention
- not too much text – enough to hold our attention.

Reading

A The Samaritans campaign ad

The Samaritans is an organization which helps people who need someone to talk to. The advertisement below and on page 66 appeared in national newspapers in 1997. As you read, think about:

- what the advertisement's main message is
- who it is aimed at
- what it tries to persuade readers to do.

Text A

SOMETIMES IT'S EASIER TO TALK TO SOMEONE YOU DON'T LIKE.

When you have a problem, it's the most natural thing in the world to want to talk it through with someone.

Sometimes, though, this creates another problem: who's the best person to confide in?

An obvious choice would be a close friend. But let's face it, we don't always choose our friends for their amazing powers of tact, diplomacy and discretion. Tell one person, and you may end up telling the world.

You may be lucky enough to be able to talk to someone in your family. Then again, you may be one of the large number of people who find talking to your nearest and dearest agonizingly embarrassing.

A girlfriend or boyfriend? If you can, great. But sometimes we don't want to expose our weaknesses to those who fancy us.

And sometimes your relationship is the very problem you want to discuss.

That's where The Samaritans can be useful. We're more discreet than your best mate, we'll listen as carefully as your girlfriend or boyfriend, and we're as sympathetic as your family. We're also non-judgemental, unshockable, and extremely experienced.

Our national number is **0345 90 90 90**, and you can e-mail us on jo@samaritans.org or visit our homepage at www.samaritans.org. We're available 24 hours a day, every day of the year.

And you don't have to be climbing up the walls before you call us – any kind of problem, big or small, is a good enough reason to pick up the phone.

Call now. You'll find we're remarkably easy to talk to.

The Samaritans
We'll go through it with you.

Text A

SOMETIMES IT'S EASIER TO TALK TO SOMEONE YOU DON'T LIKE.

If you tell your girlfriend, will she think less of you?

When you have a problem, it's the most natural thing in the world to want to talk it through with someone.

Sometimes, though, this creates another problem: who's the best person to confide in?

An obvious choice would be a close friend. But let's face it, we don't always choose our friends for their amazing powers of tact, diplomacy and discretion. Tell one person, and you may end up telling the world.

You may be lucky enough to be able to talk to someone in your family. Then again, you may be one of the large number of people who find talking to your nearest and dearest agonisingly embarrassing.

A girlfriend or boyfriend? If you can, great. But sometimes we don't want to expose our weaknesses to those who fancy us.

And sometimes your relationship is the very problem you want to discuss.

That's where The Samaritans can be useful. We're more discreet than your best mate, we'll listen as carefully as your girlfriend or boyfriend, and we're as sympathetic as your family. We're also non-judgemental, unshockable, and extremely experienced.

Our national number is **0345 90 90 90**, and you can e-mail us on jo@samaritans.org or visit our homepage at www.samaritans.org. We're available 24 hours a day, every day of the year.

And you don't have to be climbing up the walls before you call us – any kind of problem, big or small, is a good enough reason to pick up the phone.

Call now. You'll find we're remarkably easy to talk to.

The Samaritans
We'll go through it with you.

A

1 Look again at the slogan at the foot of the advertisement: 'We'll go through it with you'. Which of the statements below do you think best describes what the slogan means?

'We will explain it all clearly to you.'

'We know about suffering.'

'We will support you.'

'We're only a phone call away.'   (1 mark)

2 Say in your own words what the main heading means: 'Sometimes it's easier to talk to someone you don't like'.

(3 marks)

B

3 The advertisement gives reasons why someone may not want to discuss a problem with a close friend or a member of the family. What are they?   (4 marks)

Advice There are at least four possible points here. You don't need a separate paragraph for each one – just write one paragraph to cover all the possibilities.

4 How well does the layout of the advertisement add to its effect?   (6 marks)

Advice Look at the main image – what does it show? What do you think its message is?
Look at the slogan to the left of the box. How eye-catching is this? How does it add to the message?
Look at the way the text is organized beneath the image. What do you notice about the size of text and length of paragraphs?
Look finally at the name of the charity and the slogan. Any comments about how they are presented?

5 How does the language of the advertisement help us to feel that the Samaritans are on our side?   (6 marks)

Advice Look at the use of 'you' and 'we' in the passage.
Look at the vocabulary – why does the advertisement use words like 'mate' and 'fancy'? What does this suggest about who it is aimed at?
Is the language chiefly informal? Why? Do you notice any parts where it suddenly feels different – more formal? If so, why do you think this is?

Reading   **B** **Sight Savers campaign ad**

This advertisement is for a less well-known charity: Sight Savers International. It also appeared in national newspapers in 1997. As you read, think about:

- what the advertisement's main message is
- who it is aimed at
- what it tries to persuade readers to do.

Text B

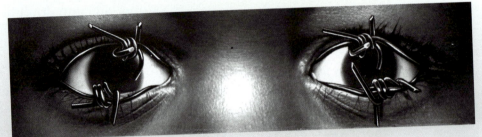

Blinking Hell

At first it's not too bad.

And it's easy to see how it's spread. Just watch a child for five minutes. They don't sit still for a moment. They're always poking their fingers into something they shouldn't, then rubbing their eyes with grubby fingers.

And that's all it takes to spread trachoma.

You only notice there's something wrong when the child's eye starts to itch and swell up

It's not terribly nice but it's bearable, and the infection will 'burn' itself out after a few weeks, leaving just a small scar on the eyelid.

The trouble is, it'll be back. And it won't just come back once. It will strike over and over again, with every reinfection burning and scarring the child's eyelids a little bit more.

In the end, after years of suffering, the eyelids become so scarred and disfigured that the eyelashes turn inwards, into the eye. Until, agonisingly slowly, you go blind.

Imagine, every time you blink, you scratch your eyes

Think about it. You've probably blinked a dozen times since you started reading this. What if you'd scratched your eyes every time? You'd be in agony and you'd be desperately trying to stop. But how do you stop blinking?

You may never even have heard of trachoma before, but 6 million people in the developing world are blind because of it. And millions more are carrying the infection. It makes life impossible for young mothers trying to raise children. Fathers and husbands can't work to support themselves, let alone their families. So the whole family suffers.

The utterly horrifying thing is, this suffering is totally unnecessary, because trachoma can be treated very quickly and cheaply in its early stages with Tetracycline ointment.

It costs as little as £1.20 to treat one person

But this is still too much for many people in the developing world, which is why we're asking you to help.

With £12 you can help relieve the suffering of ten young people with trachoma.

You can even help with the more advanced cases. £5 is all we need for the operation to turn back the ingrowing eyelashes, so they stop scratching the eye. A donation of £50 will help save the sight and relieve the suffering of ten more people.

Wouldn't you pay a hundred or a thousand times that if it were your eyes at stake? Please help by sending a donation with the coupon to:

**Sight Savers International,
FREEPOST,
Haywards Heath,
West Sussex,
RH16 3ZA**

ROYAL COMMONWEALTH SOCIETY FOR THE BLIND

A

1 Based on the advertisement, write down two facts about trachoma. (2 marks)

2 What can be used to treat trachoma quickly and effectively? (2 marks)

B

3 Comment on the main image and slogan ('Blinking Hell'). Discuss what you think the advertisers hope to achieve through them. Do you think they work? (4 marks)

Advice Write a short paragraph about the image. What does it show? How eye-catching is it? Write a short paragraph about the slogan. What does it mean? Does it catch your attention? Say whether you think the image and slogan are successful.

4 How does the advertisement use language to make the reader feel involved? (6 marks)

Advice Look at the opening sentence – how does this make us try to guess what is being described? Look at the first column. It starts with a description of a child and ends with 'you go blind'. Why does it use pronouns ('they' and 'you') in this way? Why do you think the text focuses so much on the suffering of a child?

5 The text uses phrases like 'agonisingly slowly', 'utterly horrifying', 'totally unnecessary'. Discussing each of these examples, decide what effect they have. (6 marks)

Advice Be systematic – the question is asking for a detailed response to the language. The markscheme suggests that each phrase carries two marks – make sure you write about each one. Aim to write a short paragraph (two to five sentences) about each phrase.

Writing to argue, persuade or instruct

A The Samaritans campaign ad

Imagine you are part of the advertising agency who produced the Samaritans' advertisement. When you first designed the advertisement, you needed to present it to the Samaritans organization to see what they thought about it.

Write a memo explaining what you were trying to achieve – in the image, the headings and the main text.
Set out your memo like this:

From: Your Name

To: Sam Ratcliff, Marketing Director

Date:

Subject: New newspaper ad

Dear Sam,

Here's the new ad. I hope you like it. Here's what we are trying to achieve…

Advice For practical advice on writing memos, see Self-Help Sheet 6 in the Answer Book.

B Sight Savers campaign ad

Write a fact sheet called, 'Trachoma: The Facts'.
Use it to inform people about the facts of this disease. Try to make your style factual rather than emotional. End by giving advice on what people should do to avoid developing the disease.

Advice For practical advice on writing a fact sheet, see Self-Help Sheet 7 in the Answer Book.

Biography

Introduction

Biography is writing about other people's lives. We read biographies to learn more about people we find interesting or admire, to see how they live, what their background is like, the challenges they have faced, and what makes them tick.

When we begin to read a biography we usually expect to start at the beginning of the subject's life and to follow it through to the end – either of their life, or to the point where the writer stops writing. This gives biography a strongly narrative feel: like a story, a biography usually shows us one event following another.

Biography doesn't have to be like this, and there are examples of writers trying to change the style to create a different effect. For example, the opening words of *Dickens* by Peter Ackroyd are: 'Charles Dickens was dead'. The writer recreates the scene at Dickens' death, imagining what the room where his body lay must have been like:

> '...in the dining room of Gad's Hill the curtains were pulled apart and on this June day the bright sunshine streamed in, glittering on the large mirrors round the room...'

This is the way Peter Ackroyd helps readers to enter a world that existed over a century ago: he presents it to us as if it is all there in front of our own eyes.

This unit looks at the way writers write about people. The text about Sally Gunnell is from a straightforward biography aimed at a young audience. It tells the story of its subject's life in a fairly direct way. James Mills' account of a New York detective, written in the 1960s, uses a different approach: it illuminates what a person is like by tracing a typical day in his life, while looking into his past through flashbacks.

Skills checklist

Reading biography

- Think about how much you learn about the subject's life, attitude, habits and so on.
- Comment on the way the biography is organized.
- Notice specific language features which are used by the writer to bring the subject's life alive.

Writing biography

- Research your subject's life in detail.
- Be clear from the start about how you will organize your material.
- Use language to help the reader feel involved with your subject (e.g. describing scenes in detail; imagining what was going on in your subject's mind; using dialogue to recreate what was said).

Language features

To gain higher grades at GCSE you'll need to be able to discuss the language of biography. Look out for:

- a third person narrative voice – usually 'she' or 'he' rather than 'I' or 'you'
- controlled descriptive writing to bring people and places to life
- often a narrative structure: one event leading to another, but without feeling too much like a list.

Advice panel •

- Your school or college library will have a biography section. Go and dip into opening chapters of biographies. Compare the techniques biographers use to bring subjects to life.
- Be adventurous in your thinking: biography doesn't always have to follow the same style.
- Use some of the techniques demonstrated in this unit to experiment with telling a person's life in a different style.
- Use description of people and places to bring a person's background to life.

Reading

A Sally Gunnell biography

This text is a straightforward biography of the Olympic athlete. As you read it, think about:

- what its main message is
- whether it seems factual or based on opinion
- who it is aimed at.

THE RACE

It was a hot August day in Barcelona. Eight athletes were on the starting blocks in the Olympic stadium. The track stretched out in front of them. 400 metres along the track was the finishing line. Between the athletes and the finishing line were 10 hurdles. The first athlete to cross the finishing line would win the Olympic gold medal.

'On your marks.'

In Lane 3, Sally Gunnell bent forward, her hands on the line, ready to go.

'Set.'

Suddenly, the runner in Lane 8 was off. She had started too soon. The athletes walked slowly back to the start.

Sally was behind. She was still behind at 200 metres. But by hurdle number 8, she was slightly ahead. She thought, 'You're ahead, so go for it!'

Seconds later, Sally crossed the finishing line. She had won the gold medal.

YOU ARE WHAT YOU EAT

Sally is careful about what she eats. She tries to eat good food.

She also loves going to McDonalds for a hamburger and she likes chips and chocolate. Sally bought a huge bar of chocolate to share with friends after the Olympic Final!

Athletes have to be very careful about taking medicines or herbal drinks. The rules about drug taking

Healthy food for athletes Athletes have to eat foods that give them extra vitamins and minerals.

are very tough. You can even break them by drinking too much coffee. Sally never takes any medicines for colds or headaches. Sally takes vitamin C and zinc when she gets a cold, and waits for it to get better.

THE WORLD RECORD

After the Barcelona Olympics, Sally went back to Florida in January for three weeks of hard training. Once the season started, Sally was running well. She won all her hurdles races, but the big one was coming up. This was the 400m hurdles in the World Championships at Stuttgart, Germany.

The week before the Championships, Sally caught a terrible cold. She was still coughing when she ran the first heat, and although she won the heat it was in a slow time. Sally's time in the semi-final was better, but it was only the third fastest. Sally knew she had made a mistake at the seventh hurdle.

Sally told herself, 'I've got a day's rest. I made a mistake, so I know I can run faster than that.' Sally waited for the final to start. As usual, she put everything except the race out of her mind.

Exactly 52.74 seconds later, she crossed the finishing line. The crowd were yelling and stamping. Sally looked around. Who had won? Had she won? She had, and she had broken the World Record.

Jane Coxley

A

1 Why did the 400 metre race in Barcelona have to be restarted? *(2 marks)*

2 Write down a sentence from the biography which shows that Sally Gunnell is very determined. *(2 marks)*

B

3 How can you tell that the writer of the biography admires Sally Gunnell? *(4 marks)*

Advice

Look at the way she describes her – using her first name 'Sally'.
How does she show Sally Gunnell's self-discipline?

Look at the way she also shows the human side of Sally Gunnell – find some examples.

4 How well does the writer help us to learn what Sally Gunnell is really like? *(6 marks)*

Advice

You need to show what the writer does to help us know Sally Gunnell – and you need to comment on how successful this is.
Notice how the writer shows us Sally Gunnell's thoughts.
You might comment on what we learn about the food she has to eat and the food she would like to eat. Look at the description of the Stuttgart race. How does the writer show us Sally Gunnell's feelings? Then comment on how well all of this works in showing us what Sally Gunnell is like.

5 Look at the language of the text. How can you tell that it is written for a young audience? *(6 marks)*

Advice

Look at the vocabulary – is it basic or complex?
Look at the types of sentences used – are they short and simple, or longer and complex?
Look at the style of the text. How does the writer make it feel like a story? Look at the opening sentence and the rest of the first paragraph. Are there some specific words and sentences there which make the text feel as if it is aimed at a young audience?

Reading   **B** The Detective

This text uses a very different style. It shows us what a person is like by describing them in typical situations. Here a tough New York City detective is shown with his family, then in the city, and then in flashback to his childhood. It is a style of writing we sometimes encounter in newspaper profiles of people. As you read it, think about:

- what its main message is
- whether it seems factual or based on opinion
- who it is aimed at.

THE DETECTIVE

EVERY EVENING GEORGE BARRETT KISSES HIS FOUR SONS GOODNIGHT, including the two oldest who are 17 and 19. It embarrasses the older boys to be kissed by their father, and he admits that it may seem 'a little weird.' But, he says, 'I think that the way I live I may never see them again, and I don't want to be stretched out dying in a street some place wishing for one more chance to see my family and say goodbye. So every time I kiss them it's like it's the last time I'll ever see them, and I'm kissing them goodbye forever.'

Forever can come very suddenly to Detective George Barrett. He is a hunter of men. And none of those he hunts – thieves, drug pushers, Murphy men, assault and robbery men, killers – wants to confront him on anything resembling even terms. Because when George Barrett hunts for a man, he invariably finds him; and when he finds him, the man is not always arrested, but he is always sorry he was found. George Barrett is a tough cop. His eyes, cold as gun metal, can be looked at but not into. His jaw is hard and square as a brick, and his thin lips are kept moist by nervous darting passes of his tongue. When he laughs, only his face and voice laugh. Inside, George Barrett does not laugh.

'I'm obsessed,' he says, 'with the idea that I've *got* to win, and these animals can smell it. No one's going to mess with me and win because I've been around, I've been up against the bad guys. These animals on Broadway? I'll eat them up. I've got the tools and I know how to use them. If I can't get the best of the guy with punches, I'll kick him, and if he's a better kicker than I am, I'll go with the stick or the jack, and if I have to, I'll use my gun.'

To some people George Barrett is precisely what's wrong with law enforcement. To others he is all that can save it.

In late evening darkness he stands on New York City's West 52nd Street, the 16th Precinct's northern border, and looks south into the flashing neon fireball of Times Square. This is Broadway, the Great White Way, the fabled street of dreams. Barrett calls it the sewer. Down it flows the worst America has to offer in the way of degenerates, perverts and lawbreakers – to Barrett, 'germs.'

Already on Broadway and on Seventh Avenue, down to the precinct's southern edge at 42nd Street, the prostitutes are prowling. Murphy men (confidence men who pose as pimps, then vanish when they have the money) are hunting for their marks. Car boosters, working close to the curb and nodding as they pass each car to see what they can find inside, walk the side streets, always against the traffic to thwart detectives who might follow them in squad cars. From 8 pm to midnight they'll do their biggest business, hitting theatregoers' cars, most with out-of-state plates so that the drivers will not be around to go to court if the thief is caught. No car lock can protect suitcases against the booster's screwdriver (to snap open fly windows on sedans) or his bent fork (stuck between the closed windows of a hardtop or convertible to flip up the lock button).

This early in the evening the Murphy men concentrate near the dance halls and discothèques, looking for men grown bold on beer. And looking with them are their more vicious cousins, the A&R men, assault and robbery specialists, muggers. The gypsy women, dotted around the precinct in little glass-fronted shops with dim lights, velvet chairs and phony flowers, sit seductively, moving occasionally to the doorway to invite some passer-by to taste the delicious intrigues of the back room. If the quarry enters, he will have his pocket picked, and by experts whose fingers can slip the 20s from the inside of a roll without disturbing the outside singles...

Barrett has been involved since he was 12 years old. He was living with his family in Brooklyn, and he got a brutal taste of what crime can mean. His father, a newspaper pressman, was on his way home from church when he was robbed, beaten and left for dead in a doorway. He lay there for two hours before a neighbor found him and called a doctor. Barrett remembers that the beating was so severe that 'when the doctor arrived I had to help him press on my father's stomach to keep everything in place.'

A year later young Barrett was walking behind his two brothers when he heard two thugs planning to attack them. 'I slipped into a doorway,' he says, 'and grabbed a couple of empty milk bottles. Then when the two guys started to go up on my brothers, I stepped in and tattooed them into the ground with the bottles. I did what had to be done. And ever since, that's been the story of my life. I do what has to be done.'

Barrett began his climb into the detectives' ranks on a December night in 1954, the only time he has ever shot to kill. He was a patrol-man then, off duty, on his way to visit an aunt. He heard calls for help and saw a cab driver struggling with three male passengers. Barrett approached the cab, saw a gun in the hand of one of them, and opened fire. The bullet missed,

and the passengers piled out. Barrett hit one in the mouth with his gun, shearing off the man's teeth. The other two ran. Barrett rode with the prisoner in the cab to the station house. 'I had him on the back floor of the cab with my gun in his mouth,' Barrett says, 'and he decided to tell me who his friends were.' All three admitted to 22 other stickups and burglaries – one had shot a man just the night before – and were convicted. Barrett won a promotion to detective.

A ring mark on a murdered man's finger produced Barrett's next promotion three years later. A 20-year-old ex-con named Henry Dusablon, working with a 28-year-old friend, robbed and murdered six shopkeepers in five days, four of them in one day. One of the dead men ran a novelty store in the 16th Precinct. Investigating that killing, Barrett noticed the ring mark, assumed that the ring had been stolen by the killers, and from the dead man's wife obtained a description of it. Hoping the killers would try to sell the ring, Barrett and other detectives went to work on pawnshops. They finally found the ring, pawned by Dusablon under his real name. The pawnbroker said Dusablon had known the exact weight of the stone, indicating he had already had it appraised somewhere else. The detectives canvassed other shops and finally came up with a clerk who said a man answering Dusablon's description had tried to sell him the ring. The clerk had asked him to return later and Dusablon had remarked that he was staying in a hotel nearby on West 48th Street. The detectives checked the hotels, found him, and in 1963 Dusablon and his accomplice were convicted of murder. Barrett was jumped to Detective Second Grade. He is still second grade, with a salary of $9,714.

JAMES MILLS

Word bank

> **canvassed** asked at
> **degenerates** immoral people
> **pawnbroker** a shopkeeper who gives out money in return for items
>   like jewellery and ornaments

A

1 Why might it seem 'a little weird' that George Barrett kisses his four sons goodnight each evening? (2 marks)

2 How can you tell that George Barrett does not respect the criminals he is after? (2 marks)

B

3 The text gives a clear picture of George Barrett. Write a paragraph showing what he is like – his character, his background, his attitude. Is there anything to admire about him? (6 marks)

Advice

Look at what we first learn about him – his relationship with his family.
Look at the physical description in the second paragraph. What does all this detail suggest about his character?
How have the events of his childhood affected his outlook on life?

What do you notice about the way he has made progress in his career? Then make sure you comment on whether there is anything to admire about him: does he seem a brute, or someone prepared to take on the villains? Write at least a sentence explaining your judgement.

4 How does the writer use language to create the atmosphere of downtown New York? (5 marks)

Advice

Look in particular at the middle section – 'In late evening darkness…'
Look at the visual descriptions the writer gives: what picture of the place is built up?
Look also at the way he describes

the people of the area – is he neutral in his descriptions, or critical? Look at his references to 'velvet chairs and phony flowers'. What do details like these tell you about the people and his view of them?

5 Some readers feel that the text glorifies violence. Others think James Mills shows life as it really is. Comment on the portrayal of violence in the extract. (5 marks)

Advice

How much violence is actually mentioned?
Look at the description of the events of George Barrett's childhood. Are his actions glorified? Are they presented as events which lead George Barrett to become a detective and fight crime?

Or does the writer give us more detail than we actually need about some of the violent acts – for example, shearing off a man's teeth? Use your paragraph to weigh up the two arguments. Then state what you think.

Writing to argue, persuade or instruct

A Sally Gunnell biography

Write an article for a teenage sports magazine giving advice to readers on how they should prepare themselves physically and mentally for sports competitions. Include advice about what they should eat.

Advice

For practical advice on writing articles, see Self-Help Sheet 12 in the Answer Book.

B The Detective

Imagine you have read James Mills' biography of George Barrett and you are upset by it. You feel that it glamorizes violence and shows too much interest in the low-life parts of his job.

Write to James Mills outlining your complaints against his text and stating how you think it could have been written more effectively.

Advice

To look at examples of letters see pages 109–118.
For practical advice on writing a letter, see Self-Help Sheets 4 and 5 in the Answer Book.

Reading

A **'Exercise and Fitness' information text**

This information text aims to tell readers about the positive effects of fitness and exercise. As you read it, think about:

- what its main message is
- who it is aimed at.

Text A

Enjoying
EXERCISE

Exercise is fun, and there are many ways to enjoy it. In competitive sports you can get every conceivable form of exercise. But if you don't like to compete, there are just as many leisure pursuits which will keep you in shape.

The list of activities on the right shows there are many different ways of keeping fit. While it makes sense to choose a form of exercise that improves the three key factors of suppleness, strength and stamina, there are other things to think about as well.

Activity	Suppleness	Strength	Stamina	Sociability	Economy
Archery	**	**	*	**	**
Badminton	**	**	**	**	**
Baseball	**	**	**	***	**
Basketball	**	**	***	**	**
Billiards/darts	*	--	--	**	***
Bowling	*	*	*	**	**
Boxing	**	***	***	*	**
Canoeing	**	***	**	**	*
Cricket	**	**	*	**	***
Cycling	*	***	***	**	**
Dancing (disco)	***	***	**	***	***
Fencing	***	***	**	**	**
Fishing	*	*	*	*	***
Football (soccer)	**	***	**	**	***
Football (US)	**	***	**	*	**
Golf	**	*	*	**	*
Gymnastics	***	***	*	**	**
Hiking	**	**	***	**	***
Hockey (field)	**	**	**	**	***
Hockey (ice)	***	***	***	**	*
Horse riding	*	**	*	**	*
Judo/karate	***	**	*	**	***
Mountaineering	**	***	**	**	**
Orienteering	*	**	***	**	***
Rowing	*	***	***	***	**
Rugby	*	***	**	**	***
Running	*	***	***	*	***
Sailing	*	**	*	**	*
Skating (ice)	***	**	**	**	**
Skating (roller)	***	**	**	**	***
Skiing (downhill)	***	***	**	**	*
Skipping	*	**	***	*	***
Squash	***	**	**	**	**
Surfing	**	**	*	**	**
Swimming	***	***	***	*	***
Table tennis	**	*	**	**	***
Tennis	**	***	**	**	**
Volleyball	**	***	**	**	***
Walking	*	*	**	*	***
Water skiing	*	**	**	**	*
Weight lifting	**	***	*	**	**

*** The more stars the better

You may choose a sport that brings you in contact with lots of other people, so you make new friends. You may like more solitary outdoor pursuits like orienteering, or you might prefer to take your exercise in small groups, climbing or cycling.

You are going to spend quite a lot of time carrying out your exercise programme, so choose activities that won't leave you bored after a few weeks – a mixture of different types of activity is probably best.

outdoor pursuits

Taking exercise outdoors is one of the cheapest ways to get fit and stay fit. The type of activity you take up will depend largely on the area in which you live. Jogging can be carried out almost anywhere, but if you live in a crowded city it may be safer and more enjoyable if you jog in a local park or recreation ground.

Walking is the easiest form of exercise, but to improve fitness, it should exert you enough to make you slightly breathless and to increase your pulse rate. This means a long, brisk walk, not just a comfortable stroll.

Cycling is extremely good for developing stamina and strength, but usually only the muscles of the back and legs benefit. Again it is important to keep the pace up, and this usually means extra care about road safety.

Of all types of exercise, swimming is probably the best in terms of the three key factors of suppleness, strength and stamina. And unlike many other types of exercise, you are unlikely to strain yourself by overdoing things in the early stages because your body is supported by the water.

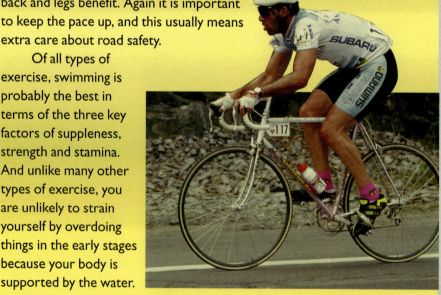

sport for health

Taking part in active sport is an enjoyable and challenging way to exercise, although the benefits depend on the type of sport involved. Team games are a popular form of exercise in schools, and they can be an important part of a fitness programme. But it is important to realize that not all team games provide the *constant* levels of aerobic exercise that are essential for improving stamina. You will need to be fairly breathless for at least 20 minutes to get real benefit.

Many team games need short bursts of exercise, rather than continuous effort. Games such as tennis and squash are ideal, because they require stamina, strength, and constant agile movement, while table tennis depends more on speed and agility.

Sports can have the disadvantage that injury is relatively common, but with proper coaching, this should not put anyone off from using sport to improve their overall fitness.

Brian R. Ward

Word bank

economy   financial cost
sociability   how much the activity lets you mix with others
stamina   how long you can keep going
suppleness   moving your muscles easily

A

1   Look at the list of activities printed on page 85 of the book and answer the questions. Name an activity which is:

   a especially good for suppleness

   b especially good for sociability

   c very good for strength, stamina and sociability

   d poor for strength and stamina

   e best overall for all categories

(5 marks)

2 Why is a mixture of activities a good idea? (2 marks)

3 Name one disadvantage of sport. (2 marks)

B

4 Write a paragraph recommending suitable activities to someone who can't see the point of exercise. (5 marks)

Advice

Think carefully about your audience – what is going to make them see the relevance of exercise?
Look at the tables of activities and the qualities each develops. Which will you stress when addressing someone who is not yet sure about exercise?
Think about how to make your language reassuring and enthusiastic about exercise.

5 Are there any clues in the language that this information text might have been written for a young audience? (6 marks)

Advice

You might not agree that this is written for a young audience – it isn't entirely straightforward.
Look at the first paragraph of the text. Do these three sentences feel simple and straightforward?
Look at the vocabulary – words like 'fun' and phrases like 'keep you in shape'. But there are also words like 'competitive' and 'conceivable'.
What do these suggest about the audience?
Look also at whether the text is telling readers new information: is it aimed at young people who don't know about exercise? Or does it seem to be aimed at readers of any age who are interested in getting fit?

Reading

B **'Aircraft Technology' information text**

This information text contains quite a lot of specific, technical information. As you read it, think about:

- what its main message is
- who it is aimed at.

Airliners

Soon after the end of the First World War, pioneers began to show the world that long distance flights across oceans could be made in safety. The excitement of fast air travel soon became attractive to business people and the wealthy, and civil airlines opened up in a number of countries. The first passenger aircraft were biplanes, two-winged aeroplanes originally designed as wartime bombers, and often built of wood and fabric.

As more and more people wanted to travel by air, purpose-built passenger aeroplanes were developed to meet demand. Many of these were monoplanes, single-winged aircraft with two or three engines, and they made regular flights between the cities of Europe and those of the United States. During the 1930s, huge four-engined flying boats became popular for long distance flights across oceans, but they could only take off and land on calm water and were not as safe as people believed. They were also slow and costly to manufacture. The modern airliner was born in the mid-1930s with the arrival of the first of the all-metal low-wing monoplanes, the Boeing 247 and the Douglas DC-2. The DC-2, and later the DC-3, proved to be faster, more reliable and more economical to operate than any of its rivals. Carrying up to 32 passengers, this aircraft helped to make air travel cheaper, and, by 1939, nine out of every ten airliners in use throughout the world were DC-3s.

Before the Second World War and for a few years after it ended, airliners were powered by piston engines and their speed was limited. Their days were soon numbered by the arrival of the jet engine. The first turbojet airliner was the de Havilland DH 106 Comet, which was put into service in 1952. With its four wing-mounted jet engines, it had a cruising speed of about 800 kph, much faster than any other airliner of the time. The Comet is considered by many to be one of the most beautiful aircraft ever built, but unfortunately it was soon beset with problems. During 1953 and 1954 two Comets broke up in mid-air, killing

American millionaire Howard Hughes on top of his own flying boat

everyone on board, and all Comets were grounded. Eventually, it was found that these accidents had been caused by weaknesses in the design of the cabin structure. In 1958 a redesigned version, the Comet 4, was put into service and remained in use until the 1970s. Since the introduction of the Comet, the basic design and appearance of the airliners have changed very little.

The Comet was followed by the Boeing 707, the first of a long and highly successful family of aircraft. Other turbojets included the Douglas DC-8 and the Sud-Aviation Caravelle. The Caravelle had two engines mounted on the fuselage near the tail, allowing the wing to operate with greatest efficiency.

By now, all long range airliners were designed, like the Comet, to cruise at altitudes between 6,000 and 12,000 metres. At this height, not only is the air calmer, making flight more comfortable for the passengers, but the engines and wings can operate at the highest efficiency. Above a height of about 2,500 metres, the pressure of the atmosphere falls rapidly, and for passenger comfort the cabin has to be pressurized, and kept pumped up by electric motors to a pressure to which people are accustomed on the ground.

This calls for an airtight cabin with a cross-section which is circular. Smaller passenger aircraft that do short journeys and cruise at lower heights can have fuselages that are box-shaped since the cabins do not need to be pressurized.

The more passengers an airliner can carry, the more economic it usually becomes, and the cheaper it is to fly. The year 1969 saw the first of the big wide-bodied jet airliners, the Boeing 747, which can carry between 320 and 500 passengers. It was followed by other wide-bodied airliners, such as the McDonnell Douglas DC-10, the Lockheed 1011 Tristar, and the Airbus Industrie A300B.

Among the latest airliners is the wide-bodied Boeing 747-400. This has a fully computerized, digital cockpit that can be operated by a flying crew of two. A flight engineer is no longer needed, since engine performance is continually monitored by computer. It has advanced engines that consume less fuel and the aircraft can fly about 13,000 km without refuelling. All these factors help to reduce the cost of long-distance air travel.

Smaller airliners, such as the Boeing 757 and 767, are also equipped with digital cockpits. The Airbus A320 is equipped with the latest avionics and fly-by-wire systems. Nearly all of this

A Boeing 747

Cockpit of a Boeing 737-300

aircraft's functions are electronically controlled, involving over fifteen different interlinked computers. A centralized fault display system flashes up faults on a screen near the pilots. This system will soon be modified so that details of faults can be signalled to the ground. By the time the aircraft lands, ground engineers will have plans ready for repair work to begin immediately.

Supersonic flight

As an aircraft moves through the air, pressure waves move out in front of it. These travel at the speed of sound (about 1,220 kph). When the aircraft reaches the speed of sound, the pressure waves 'pile up' in front of it. The increase in pressure has the result of creating shock waves. These build up on various parts of the aircraft, including the leading and trailing edges of the wings.

In generating lift, the air above the wing travels faster than the aircraft itself. When the aircraft is travelling at very nearly the speed of sound, the air above the wing may actually be moving at a supersonic speed. The flow pattern of the air becomes more turbulent as the speed of sound is reached. Once the aircraft exceeds the speed of sound (Mach 1), it is said to pass through the sound barrier. The aircraft overtakes the pressure waves and the shock waves form a cone that spreads out behind it. As the shock waves pass over the ground below, a dull sonic boom is heard.

All aircraft that fly at supersonic speeds are designed to pierce the pressure waves with the least amount of drag. The nose must be pointed and the wings have to be tapered. In appearance, a supersonic aircraft is shaped like a paper dart.

Mark Lambert

Word bank

avionics   use of electronics in aviation
fuselage   body of aeroplane

A

1   When did long-distance flights by air begin to be made?

(2 marks)

2   Name one of the first modern airliners.   (2 marks)

3   Why is it important that an aircraft should carry as many passengers as possible?   (2 marks)

B

4   What have been the main stages in the development of aircraft from the First World War to the present day? Write your answer as a list of numbered points.   (5 marks)

Advice

Look at aircraft made at the end of the First World War – what were they like?
Look at the flying boats of the 1930s. The text says these were 'popular' but 'slow and costly'. Should you include them in your list?

Look at stages which then move the aircraft from the mid-1930s to the present day.
Don't feel that you need to give much detail about each type of aeroplane – you are being assessed on your ability to spot the different stages of development.

5   Look at the panel about supersonic flight. Draw a diagram and label it to show readers how supersonic flight works. Then write about how clear you found the information to follow.   (4 marks)

Advice

Don't spend too long on the details of the illustration. Your drawing skills are not being tested here. Feel free to do a very quick first draft. Label it with a subheading

'Planning'. Then just cross it out with a single line.
Use your labels, with arrows, to show the reader how supersonic flight works.

6   Comment on the language of the extract. How clear is it? How well does it take complicated ideas and present them simply? How could the extract be improved?   (4 marks)

Advice

Express your own opinion here – just make sure you support your

points with specific reference to the language.

Finish your answer with suggestions about how the text might be improved – either in terms of design and layout, or organization of material, or clarity of language.

Writing to argue, persuade or instruct

A 'Exercise and Fitness' information text

Using the information from the information book, put together a leaflet for teenagers encouraging them to get more actively involved in sport and fitness activities. Stress all the advantages this will bring. Use headings, images (sketch these roughly) and language to persuade your reader to become more active. Remember your young audience – keep the tone light and informal.

Advice

To look at examples of leaflets see pages 10-26.
For practical advice on creating a leaflet, see Self-Help Sheet 1 in the Answer Book.

B 'Aircraft Technology' information text

Imagine a local museum has a section on aircraft technology. They ask you to produce a one-side fact sheet giving the history of aircraft aimed at a young audience of 8-12 year olds.

Design your fact sheet using headings, images (sketch these roughly), and text to inform your audience.

Advice

For practical advice on writing a fact-sheet, see Self-Help Sheet 7 in the Answer Book.

Advertorials

We usually think about advertising as something which is fairly direct – commercials on television, jingles on the radio and slogans in newspapers and magazines. A lot of advertising is like this, but there are other styles too.

This unit looks at less direct forms of advertising, which are sometimes called 'advertorials'. These are advertisements which appear in newspapers and magazines and look, at first glance, like articles. Usually in small print above them they actually say 'advertisement' so that the reader knows that they are intended to promote or sell a product.

This kind of advertising can be very powerful. It presents information about a product in a format that is factual. We read newspaper articles to find out about things that have (usually) really happened; so to present information about a product in this way can make the reader treat it more seriously than they would a traditional advertisement.

This kind of advertising isn't 'cheating'. It doesn't aim to mislead or confuse the reader. Instead, it is using the layout and language of newspapers to promote a product – and usually to give more information than might otherwise be possible.

Reading advertorials
- Recognize the features of both newspapers and advertising which are being used.
- Comment on the use of language and layout.
- Discuss the message which the advertiser is hoping to communicate.

Writing advertorials
- Think carefully about the message you wish to communicate.
- Work out the best format and style for this.
- Construct your text so that the reader wants to keep reading it: it therefore needs a lively style as well as information about a product.

To gain higher grades at GCSE you'll need to be able to discuss the language of advertorials. Look out for:

- the language features of newspapers – short paragraphs, snappy style, subheadings; plus:

- the language features of advertising – lots of references to the product, the benefits it will bring, good service, and so on.

The early part of the advertorial is likely to feel most like a newspaper article; the later parts are likely to feel most like an advertisment.

Advice panel •

- Try to get familiar with advertorials – look out for them in newspapers and magazines.
- To analyse and write them well, you need to have a good understanding of how newspaper and magazine articles are written. Get into the habit of reading a daily paper. Try to look beyond what the stories are about and focus on the writers' style.

Reading

A Norwich Union Direct advertorial

This advert is written in the style of two tabloid newspaper articles. As you read it, think about:

- who it is aimed at
- what its main message is
- what it tries to persuade readers to do.

THE SUN, Tuesday, November 4 1997

ADVERTIS

Text A

Aisle save £250 o

By SHIRLEY BLACK

BOOST FOR BRIDE LOU

WHEN beautiful bride Louise White walked down the aisle in her fairytale wedding dress the last thing on her mind was the cost of car insurance.

But the 23-year-old got an unexpected gift from Norwich Union Direct when she went to buy her first car.

Louise had set her heart on a new SEAT Ibiza 1.4SE but was afraid of high insurance premiums.

Her wedding to 25-year-old recruitment consultant Robert meant she had little spare cash.

But Norwich Union Direct came up with the answer to her problems.

Helpful

Louise, of Worthing, Sussex, says: 'I saw the car one Saturday in June and wanted to get on the road really quickly.

'I rang around five or six companies and couldn't believe it when the quote from Norwich Union Direct was £250 cheaper than one of the other companies.

'They were very helpful on the phone and allowed me to pay monthly premiums.

'After all the expense of the wedding this was really useful.

'I was able to drive off in my new car just two days later.'

Louise pays 10 monthly payments of £25.38 having paid two premiums in advance to give her fully comprehensive cover. She adds: 'I was amazed that there could be such a price difference between the various companies.'

'The quote from Norwich Union Direct even beat the one offered by SEAT.'

Now Louise uses her car every day for the 25-mile round trip to Brighton where she works as a mortgage finance advisor.

She says: 'This is the first time I have run my own car for about three years.

'When I last owned one, I built up some no-claims bonus and Norwich Union Direct were the only one of the companies I contacted who agreed to take this into account.'

To see how much you could save on your car insurance, call Norwich Union Direct free on 0800 888 111. Remember to have your car registration number handy.

Norwich Union Direct motor customers enjoy great cover at excellent rates.

And that's not all. There's also the option to add Protection Plus breakdown cover, including At Home service and roadside recovery, backed by the RAC from just £45 a year.

New and existing Norwich Union Direct motor insurance customers can easily add this valuable cover with just one call.

Phone free on 0800 888 111 for more details. Again make sure your car registration number is available.

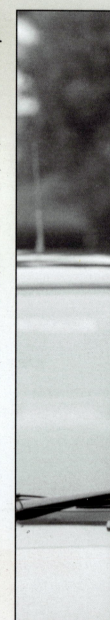

STEER-LY IN L

car cover

END GUY FAWKES THIEVES

REMEMBER, remember, the fifth of November is one of the busiest nights of the year for burglars.

Guy Fawkes night means rich pickings for homebreakers because people are out at fireworks parties.

And the sound of forced entry is masked by the noise.

Here are some tips from leading insurer Norwich Union Direct to ward them off:

● A visible burglar alarm may make thieves think twice – and reduce your insurance premiums.

● Fit deadlocks to doors which meet British Standards.

● Leave lights on and curtains closed when going out at night. Timer switches are also a good idea.

● Never leave spare keys in an obvious place.

● Secure sheds and garages – especially if they contain tools that could be used to break in.

● Two out of three burglars gain access through windows so it's a good idea to fit window locks.

● Mark valuable items in indelible ink with your postcode to help the police return stolen goods to you.

● Photograph expensive items and keep a list of serial or registration numbers.

● The safety of your area can be considerably enhanced by joining a Neighbourhood Watch Scheme.

Membership can make your home a lower insurance risk – which could mean lower premiums for you.

Call free on 0800 888 222.

newly-wed Louise was thrilled with saving

A

1 How has Louise White saved £250? (2 marks)

2 In what ways does this advertising feature *look* like a newspaper article? (4 marks)

Advice There are four marks available for this question. Try to make four quick points.

B

3 Read the first five paragraphs. At what point do you think a reader would realize that the text was an advertisement feature? Explain your answer. (4 marks)

4 Look at the right-hand column headlined 'End Guy Fawkes Thieves'. Why do you think this feature has been included? (4 marks)

Advice The main text aims to inform the reader about an event that has happened. How does the 'Guy Fawkes' article feel different? Why would the writer wish to include advice like this? What might she or he be hoping that the reader will think by the end of the section?

5 The advertorial 'Aisle Save £250...' certainly *looks* like a newspaper article. Does it also read like one? Write a paragraph or more discussing the style of the text – ways in which it does feel like a newspaper article and ways in which it doesn't. (6 marks)

Advice Look at the headline and subheading – do these seem like real newspaper style? Look at the use of the image with the caption below ('Steer-ly in love'). Does this help the text seem like a genuine newspaper article? Notice the fact that the writer's name is given (Shirley Black). You wouldn't find this in direct advertising. What is the effect? The name of the company, Norwich Union Direct, is mentioned several times in the extract. What effect does this have? Does the end of the text feel any different in style from the beginning? You might organize your answer into two paragraphs – one about ways in which the text does feel like a newspaper article and the other about ways in which it doesn't. Remember to support your points with specific examples.

B Memory and Concentration Studies advertorial

This advert looks like a newspaper article, but its style is different. As you read it, think about:

- who it is aimed at
- what its main message is
- how it is similar to or different from a real newspaper article.

Text B

Why Does Your Memory Fail You?

A **WORLD-FAMOUS** memory expert, who has trained industrialists, trades unionists, businessmen, professional men, salesmen, housewives and students to improve their memories, once said:

'Many people are embarrassed by a poor memory, and find difficulty in concentrating; whilst others realize that they lose business, academic and social opportunities not only because they cannot remember accurately everything they see, hear or read, but also because they cannot think or express their thoughts clearly, logically and concisely. Some seek advice, but many do not, mainly because they believe their memories cannot be improved.'

Forget names, faces?

Simple Technique

And yet, he went on to explain, he has devised a simple technique which can improve even the poorest memory. What's more, it can even work like magic to give you added poise, self-confidence and greater personal effectiveness. Everyone owes it to himself to find out more about this method.

Rapid Results

According to this remarkable man, anyone – regardless of his present skill – could, in just 20 minutes a day, improve his memory and concentration to a remarkable degree. For example, you need never forget another appointment – ever! You could learn names, faces, facts, figures and foreign languages faster than you ever thought possible. You may be able to imprint whole books on your memory after a single reading. You could be more successful in your studies and examinations. At parties and dinners you may never again be at a loss for appropriate words or entertaining stories. In fact, you could even be more poised and self-confident in everything you say and do.

Free

To acquaint all readers of The Independent with the easy-to-follow rules for developing skill in remembering, we, the publishers, have printed full details of this interesting self-training method in a fascinating book, 'Adventures in Memory', sent free on request. No obligation. No salesman will call. Just fill in and return the coupon on Page (you don't even need to stamp your envelope), or write to:- Memory and Concentration Studies (Dept. IDM 37), FREEPOST 198, Manchester M60 3DL.

Comparison by theme

Introduction

When studying English at GCSE level, you are expected to be able to compare texts, both during the course and in many of the examination questions which are set. Check with your teacher for more details of the exact requirements.

Comprehension to GCSE gives you a number of opportunities to compare texts within a similar genre – for example, comparing newspaper articles or leaflets.

Sometimes you might be given texts which belong to different genres but are linked by theme. This unit prepares you for that possibility. It contains two different types of text, but both are on the theme of personal computing.

Text A is a piece of personal writing by Adam Woodyatt who plays Ian Beale in *EastEnders*. He writes about his interest in computers. Text B is from an information booklet produced by the electrical store Comet. It aims to tell readers more about the Internet.

The questions which follow the texts encourage you to compare and contrast them. *Compare* means spotting what they have in common. *Contrast* means spotting how they are different.

Skills checklist

Reading the texts
- Understand what is being said in both texts.
- Notice the way each text is written.
- Notice the similarities and differences between the style of the texts.

Language features
- Autobiographical writing is likely to be more personal: watch out for the pronouns 'I' and 'me'.
- You are also likely to be learning about what the writer is like – his interests, attitudes and enthusiasms.
- The information text is likely to be more impersonal – though that doesn't mean it has to be boring or stuffy. It may use the pronoun 'you' to make the reader feel involved.
- Expect more detailed information in the second text – facts about computers, modems, the Internet and so on.
- Expect the second text also to use layout features seen in leaflets and information books – short paragraphs, bullet-points, headlines, and subheadings.

Comparison

Magazine review and information text

As you read these two texts, think about how they differ, in terms of:

- who they are aimed at
- what their messages are
- what they try to persuade readers to do.

Text A

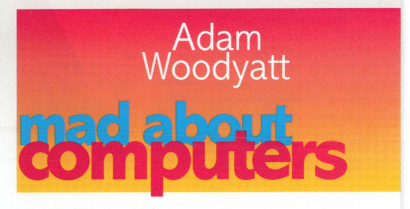

Adam Woodyatt

mad about computers

I'M 28 AND I RECKON I was the last generation not to do computer studies at school, but I remember being fascinated when the first home computers appeared in the shops. I'd go in and press keys and watch things scroll up and down, but I didn't have a clue what I was doing. When I joined the cast of *EastEnders* at 16 and started earning my own money, I went out and bought my first computer to play games on. In those days, the games came on tapes which you had to load into the computer from a tape recorder. It was a very long and boring process so you had to be dedicated – and I was!

My next step up was an Amiga computer which frightened the life out of me at first, because I knew what I wanted it to do but I couldn't communicate with it. Also, I had to get the hang of using a mouse. I was still really only playing games, but I gradually became aware of all the things that the computer could do, like word-processing and desktop publishing, and I found that the more I played with it the more I could make it do.

Then there was the Great Leap Forward when I began producing a newsletter for the Walford Boys' Club, the *EastEnders* cast football team. At

first the only way I could get photos in was to photocopy them and stick them in with glue, but then someone lent me an old security video camera with a digitiser [which transfers photos into a computer], so I could put the pictures on the page before it was printed.

When I got my present PC in 1991, I remember it crashed and died four times before I got the hang of it. But the good news is that these days the new operating systems do everything for you. You just point the mouse to what you want, click, and you've got it. And if you're about to make a mistake, the computer says 'Are you sure?' – and you say 'No!'

I still enjoy playing games on my computer, but I use it for lots of other things, too. One of my favourite bits of software lets me play film director – it allows you to choose the dialogue and camera angles and move the actors around. I write all my letters on the computer and quite often I mail them by computer as well, using e-mail.

Just before Christmas, I took the plunge and joined the Internet. It's quite addictive. If there's nothing decent on telly and the family are asleep, I'll spend a couple of hours 'talking' to people around the world. It's made me realize that the whole world is an actor because no one says what they really do for a living, including me. If I let on that I was Ian Beale, my e-mail would go ballistic!

There really is no limit to what you can get on the Internet. It's like the world's biggest library, shopping catalogue, car supermarket and holiday company rolled into one.

It's incredible to think that the modern personal computer has more processing power than the one that sent the first spacecraft to the moon. Like most people, I only use a fraction of my computer's capabilities, but I do a bit more with it every year. Once there's a computer in your life, the only limit is your pocket! ■

Mad about computers

Why do I need the Internet?

Getting on-line to the Internet means hooking up your PC to thousands of other computers all over the world. So far, over 30 million people have joined – and you can too – this guide from Comet and What PC? tells you all you need to know. Once you're connected you'll find there's plenty to do...

- Download software to use on your own computer. Much of it is free and you can also get trial versions of the latest commercial releases.
- Use electronic mail to send messages to anybody else on the Internet; it's faster (and cheaper) almost always than by ordinary post or telephone.
- Make new friends by looking in on newsgroups. These exist for every type of hobby and activity and many of the groups hold regular meetings in real life, too. Whether you're into Bull Terriers, Bonsai trees, International peace or Star Trek memorabilia, there's a group you can join to meet other people with similar interests.
- Keep up-to-date. You can read all the latest news from *The Times*, *The Daily Telegraph* and other national and international newspapers and magazines. For motoring information you can log on to Vauxhall's traffic congestion maps, updated every three minutes, courtesy of Trafficmaster. There are weather reports,

sports results, book reviews, movie guides and much more.

- Go shopping on the Internet. You can order wine, chocolates, flowers and gift vouchers from shops like Sainsbury's – or buy anything from clothes, holidays, books and CDs to car insurance, all available from the host of on-line suppliers. Let Admiral quote for your car insurance renewal on the Internet and you even qualify for an extra discount.
- Make business contacts. Thousands of companies advertise on the Internet, and so can you: it costs nothing.

All this is just the start, because the Internet is growing daily as more people and companies join in. Planned improvements in the means of making payments over the Internet, either by credit card or

http//www.sky.

http//202.78.2

through a personal account, mean that you'll soon have a wider choice of goods and services than any single shopping centre could ever provide, as well as free access to more information than the biggest libraries in the world.

how the internet works

Let's say you've hooked up your home PC to the Internet; this means you are connected, via your phone line, to a computer belonging to your Internet service provider. If, for example, you wanted to know how far it is from your home to Sydney, in Australia, there's a computer at the University of Michigan which can tell you. You don't have to call the States to get information from the computer in Michigan. You only pay for the local call to your service provider who makes the connection to Michigan across the Internet and relays the information to you.

The effect is the same as if you had

connected to Michigan yourself, but you don't have to worry about the complexities of how computers communicate with each other – you just point and click on your PC.

The Internet is a big place, but most people find they can do everything they want to do using just three of its services; the World Wide Web, E-Mail and newsgroups.

what is the world wide web?

The World Wide Web (often written as WWW and called 'The Web') is the most popular part of the Internet. It's where people and organizations display information for everybody to see. The colourful pages of the Web use words, pictures and sounds to get their message across. Companies use it to provide information about themselves and their products, and even to sell some of them directly. Other organizations, both public and private, use it to spread information of general interest, and individuals tend to advertise themselves or promote causes they're particularly interested in.

Finding your way around the Web is easy. There are parts of it devoted to searching where you can type in a subject you're interested in and get back a list of all the computers, wherever they are in the world, holding information on the topic you're looking for.

The software you use while you're on the Web is called a browser. This is an apt name because many of the pages on the Web contain links to other pages. If you click on a link you are quickly transferred to another page on another computer. In this way you can browse your way all round the world just by clicking with your mouse. It's amazing what you can find while you're 'surfing' around like this. ■

ttp//www.sky.co.uk

http//202.78.2.

A

1 Write down one fact from the first text. (2 marks)

2 Write down one fact from the second text. (2 marks)

3 Write down one opinion from the first text. (2 marks)

4 Write down one opinion from the second text. (2 marks)

Advice This is more difficult – but there are some opinions there. Look for sentences which tell you about how you will *feel* once you connect to the Internet.

B

5 How do the two texts reassure someone that using a computer is straightforward and not frightening? (6 marks)

Advice Look at the tone of Adam Woodyatt's writing in text A: how does he make computing sound easy and fun? Look at the vocabulary he uses to make it seem straightforward.
Look at how text B plays down the technical details of the Internet and encourages the reader to think of the creative possibilities. Look at how it appeals to a range of possible users. Look at how it keeps its language fairly informal and reassuring.

6 The two texts belong to different genres (types of writing). What do you notice about the language of text A which is typical of personal writing, and what do you notice about the language of text B which makes it seem typical of an information text? (6 marks)

Advice Look at the informal style of text A. Find examples of the way words have been compressed to make them more chatty, and where everyday words are used in place of more formal vocabulary.
Look at what we learn about the writer. Look at the way the writer sometimes uses exclamation marks at the ends of sentences to give them an informal style.
Look at the way 'I' is used throughout the text.
With text B look at the use of the pronoun 'you'. What effect does this have?
Look at ways in which the writer has given the text a more informal feel. Look at how technical information is made simple.
Look out for words like 'amazing' and 'easy'. What effect do they have?
Look at the layout features of the text – how are these typical of information texts?

I'm afraid there isn't nearly as much time for writing letters as I thought, owing to this awful spit & polish, but we find time in the evenings all right at the moment.

Are you sending my sweet ration card on, because I must have it soon as Sergeant has asked for it. We have been very lucky with our N.C.Os & they are all strict but very sweet & human, one especially who is a canadian & was six months in the star demonstration platoon touring the country.

Lights out are just going & so I must stop, but I will try & ring you up tomorrow.

Lots of love & kisses
Lucia

Word bank

> **exalted**   high
> **NCO**   non-commissioned officer
> **sweet ration card**   during the War sugar was in short supply, like many other commodities. Ration cards were issued to try to ensure that everyone received the same amount.

A

1 Even before you read this text in detail, you can see that it is a letter. Write down three clues that show you.   (3 marks)

2 What is the writer finding almost unbearable?   (3 marks)

B

3 How would you describe the tone of the letter – is it cheerful, upset, angry, worried? Choose a word (either your own or one of these) which best describes the tone and write a sentence supporting your choice.   (4 marks)

Advice   You can choose your own word to describe the tone.
Remember that 'tone' is the writer's emotional mood.

Other possible words to describe tone: serious, nervous, disgruntled (= unhappy with conditions), resigned (= accepting that she

cannot change anything).
Be sure to support your chosen
word with a precise example – not
just a quotation. You need to write
in your own words about the word
you have chosen.

4 **What picture do you gain of the writer from her letter?**
Write a paragraph about her personality.   (5 marks)

Advice

Any hints about her social class or
background?
Look at the way she addresses her
mother.
Look at the way she signs off – what
does this suggest about her and her
relationship with her mother?
Look for clues to her relationships
with others.
Notice her comment about
promotion – what type of
personality does this suggest?

5 **How can you tell from the language that this is an informal**
letter – written from one person to someone she knows
well?   (5 marks)

Advice

Look at the way the date is written.
Look at the way she starts and signs
off the letter.
Notice the verb forms: wouldn't 'I
am' be much more formal than 'I'm'?
Look at the way sentences are
joined together: what kind of feel
does this give the text?
Look at the vocabulary – is it chatty
or formal?

Reading

B **Save the Children letter**

This public letter is part of a campaign to raise support for the
Save the Children charity. It therefore has features of both
letters and advertising. As you read, think about:

- what impression you get of the author
- who the letter is aimed at
- what its message is.

Text B

Save the Children

Mary Datchelor House, 17 Grove Lane, Dept. 7050243, London SE5 8RD.
(Registered Charity No. 213890)

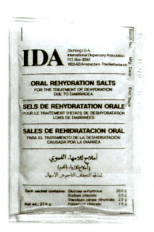

Over 8,000 children die from dehydration every day. But a simple solution of clean water, salt and sugar – provided in a small sachet like the one you see here – is all it takes to save them.

Just 7p is all that keeps Erisa from a death that will claim more than 3 million children this year.

Dear Friend,

   Each day as you read your newspaper or watch the television you'll hear of people fleeing a new disaster. It may be a war, a famine or a flood. But you can be certain that it is the children who will suffer most.

   All over the world, displaced and refugee children like Erisa are suffering from dehydration - a condition caused by acute diarrhoea which claims the lives of more than 3 million children every year.

But these children are dying needlessly.

   With your help, Save the Children can alleviate the plight of these refugee children. Because a simple solution of sugar, salt and water is all it takes to reverse the lethal effects of dehydration and give these children a much better chance of survival.

   This life-saving solution is easily available in ready-mixed small sachets, pictured above, which cost just 7p.

   But still children are dying. Because without trained workers in

Please read on...

their communities, we have no way of ensuring little children like Erisa get the simple medicine they so desperately need.

I'd like to share Erisa's story with you and that of her sister Celestine, who at the age of fourteen became responsible for looking after her little sister.

Living in a camp and left to care for her family, young Celestine learned what it takes to survive.

When political killings swept Rwanda, Celestine and her family had to flee their home so quickly they could only take the bare essentials - what little food they had and the clothes on their backs. A long and fearful trek brought them to a camp on the side of a hill, where hundreds of other displaced families were already settled in.

Their makeshift home was made from plastic sheeting. Water supplies and sanitation were so poor that disease threatened every child in the camp. Here Celestine, her three brothers and baby sister lived on the little their father could earn.

But despite these hardships, Celestine faced an even greater challenge.

Her mother was ill. While her father struggled to find work, this left 14-year-old Celestine with the adult responsibility of caring for the other children.

Celestine's baby sister Erisa became sick.

Diarrhoea wracked Erisa's body. Left long enough she would have become severely dehydrated and malnourished, leading to a painful death.

Fortunately for Erisa, there was a health centre nearby supported by Save the Children. The centre was abandoned when the massacre spread, and most of its medicines were looted. When some local health workers were able to return, they could do very little with the few drugs available. But now Save the Children had re-stocked the centre with medicines and were training more staff to cope with the rising need. So now a nurse was able to visit Erisa and give her the care she needed.

Over the course of a day Erisa was given a solution from a sachet of ready-mixed rehydration salts to stop the dehydration.

It was a sachet just like the one in the photograph. The nurse also showed Celestine how to make her own rehydration solution out of sugar and salt - and give her sister a much better chance of survival.

Like most families in her situation, Celestine had no measuring

Please read on...

Text B

equipment. Too much salt in the solution could be lethal to a child in Erisa's condition. So the nurse explained to Celestine how the solution should taste, and how Celestine could easily check for herself by tasting a very small amount.

Celestine was also taught about preventing illness and how boiling water and washing kills the germs that made Erisa so ill.

Of course, Celestine will never know whose donation paid for the rehydration salts that saved her sister's life. <u>Nor can she know how little 7p seems to you and I compared to the value it has in saving a child's life.</u>

It is through the continued support of people like you that Save the Children is able to help treat children like Erisa.

And treating symptoms is only half the story. Save the Children also trains the people in refugee camps to feed and protect their children – so the difference your donations make actually lasts. **But this long term work needs regular support.**

<u>Will you pledge a small monthly gift to Save the Children? Every penny you can spare will help protect an innocent child from unfair deprivation.</u>

On behalf of Celestine, Erisa and all the other children who fill the world's refugee camps today – thank you for taking a moment to read this letter. And thank you for your support.

Yours sincerely,

A. Timpson

Andrew Timpson
Save the Children Africa Programme Officer.

PS. Remember, as little as £2 could help save 30 children from the fatal effects of dehydration – <u>every month.</u> Please pledge whatever you can today. Thank you.

Your Donation Form is printed overleaf.

Word bank

> **acute** severe
> **alleviate** help, relieve
> **dehydration** lack of water in the body
> **displaced** homeless
> **wracked** tortured

A

1 In what ways does the text look like a letter? (2 marks)

2 In what ways does it *not* look like a letter? (2 marks)

3 Say in one sentence what you think the main purpose of the letter is. (2 marks)

B

4 This is a long letter, and it is important that the writer manages to hold our attention. How successfully does the writer use layout to keep us interested? (6 marks)

Advice

Look at the start of the letter. What effect does the picture of the rehydration sachet have in capturing our attention?
Look at the headline. How does the writer make it stand out? What effect does this have?
Notice the length of paragraphs – why are they short?

Look at the use of underlining, subheadings, and bold text throughout the letter. What do you notice about the way the writer uses these?
How successfully overall do you think the writer uses layout? How could the layout be improved?

5 The writer hopes that we will become emotionally involved in the dreadful conditions he describes and will become regular supporters of Save the Children's work. What techniques are used to persuade us to help, and how successful overall do you find the letter? (8 marks)

Advice

Comment on the use of 'Dear Friend' at the start of the letter and also the pronoun 'you' – how is this trying to get the reader involved?
Look more closely at Celestine and Erisa's story. How does the writer make us feel an emotional reaction to what he describes? Look at the words used to describe their conditions.

What impression does the writer create of the work Save the Children does in Rwanda? How does he make us feel sympathetic to their cause? Why does the writer keep stressing the cost of 7p?
Look at the way the writer concludes the letter 'On behalf of Celestine, Erisa and all the other children who fill the world's refugee

camps...'. What effect does this have?

How does the end of the letter try to convert our emotional response into active help (by donating money)?

Remember to comment on how successful overall the letter is. If there are parts that don't work for you, say so – just explain why.

Writing to argue, persuade or instruct

 A Wartime letter

Lucia Lawson complains about the attitude and behaviour of some of the people around her. What do you suppose they think of her? Imagine you are one of them, and write a letter home in which you show how you have settled in and, in particular, your first impressions of Lucia Lawson.

Use your own name, if you wish, and address your letter 'Dear Mother'.

Advice   For practical advice on writing letters, see Self-Help Sheets 4 and 5 in the Answer Book.

 B Save the Children letter

Create an advertising leaflet about the suffering caused by dehydration and show what a dramatic effect the rehydration sachets can have. Aim to show readers what they should do to help and persuade them to support the Save the Children cause.

Use layout and language to make your reader take notice of your message.

Advice   To look at examples of leaflets see pages 10-26.
For practical advice on creating a leaflet, see Self-Help Sheet 1 in the Answer Book.

Acknowledgements

The publishers would like to thank the following for permission to reproduce photographs:

Allsport: pp 73, 74; Ardea/Adrien Warren: p 32 (left); Yann Arthus-Betrand/Corbis: p 63; Colorific/Telegraph Colour Library: p 113; Corbis-Bettmann: p 89; Corel Professional Photos: pp 14 (top left & top right), 86, 87, 90; Express Newspapers: p 31; Eye Ubiquitous/Corbis: p 42; Getty Images/Hulton: p 111; Getty Images/Tony Stone/Amwell: p 84 (left); Getty Images/Tony Stone/Matthew McVay: p 84 (right); Kit Houghton Photography/Corbis: p 30; Image Bank: pp 47, 52 (both), 53; Bob Krist/Corbis: pp 55, 56; Popperfoto: p 32 (right); Roger Ressmeyer/© Corbis: p 91; Retrograph Archive Ltd: p 95; Rex Features: p 104 (top); Telegraph Colour Library: p 104 (bottom); Penny Tweedie/Corbis: p 60; UPI/Corbis-Bettmann: pp 49, 76, 77, 78, 79.

The author and publisher are grateful to the following for permission to reprint copyright material:

BBC Learning Support for Adam Woodyatt: 'Mad About Computers' first published by BBC Education in *Computers Don't Bite*, May 1997; Comet Group for extract from 'Why do I need the Internet?' in *The What PC & Software Guide to the Internet*, Comet Retail store leaflet, July 1997; Express Newspapers plc for Tony Brooks: 'Helicopter dash saves dive twins' from *The Express* 10.11.97, and Lynne Wallis: 'Different classes who are brought together by the thrill of the chase'/'In hot pursuit, saboteurs on the hunt's trail' from 'Life', *The Express* 4.11.97; Ginn & Company for extract from Jane Coxley: *Sally Gunnell* (Ginn, 1995), Copyright © 1995; Greenpeace for extracts from leaflet, 'Actions Speak Louder', Copyright © Greenpeace; R & W Heap (Publishing) Company Ltd for advertisement for *Memory and Concentration Studies*; A M Heath & Co Ltd on behalf of the Estate of George Orwell for extract from George Orwell: 'Shooting an Elephant' (Secker & Warburg Ltd, 1955), Copyright © Mark Hamilton as the Literary Executor of the Estate of the Late Sonia Brownell Orwell; David Higham Associates for extract from Michael Asher: *A Desert Dies* (Viking, 1986); Ewan MacNaughton Associates on behalf of the Telegraph Group Ltd for Barbie Dutter: 'Pilot flies below bridges to save divers', and graphic from *The Daily Telegraph* 10.11.97; Macmillan for entry on Florence Nightingale from *Macmillan Encyclopaedia* (Macmillan Reference Books, 1981); Northcote House Educational Publishers for David Swift: 'Cursed' from *Out of Sight* edited by Stephen Humphries and Pamela Gordon (Channel 4/Northcote House 1992); Norwich Union for extract from 1997 advertisement feature; Oxford University Press for entry on Florence Nightingale from the *Oxford Children's Encyclopedia* edited by Ben Dupré (1996); RSPCA for extracts from leaflet, 'Flung against a wall' (created by Brann Ltd, Bristol); The Rough Guides for extract from Kate Pullinger: 'Hitching Through the Yukon' in *Women Travel* edited by Miranda Davies and Natania Jansz (Rough Guides, 1990); The Samaritans for 1997 advertisement; Save the Children Fund for 1997 campaign letter; Sight Savers International for 'Blinking Hell' advertisement; Tesco Stores Ltd for extracts from 'Healthy Eating for Children' leaflet; Time Life for extracts from James Mills: 'The Detective' first published in *Life* Magazine 12.3.65; Waitrose Ltd for extracts from 'Eating and Good Health' leaflet; The Watts Publishing Group for extracts from Brian R Ward: *Lifeguides: Exercise and Fitness* (first published in the UK by Franklin Watts, a division of the Watts Publishing Group, 96 Leonard Street, London EC2A 4RH, 1988); Wayland Publishers for extracts from Mark Lambert: *Technology in Action: Aircraft Technology* (Wayland, 1989); The Hon. Mrs L Whitehead for Lucia Lawson letter published in *Letters in Wartime* edited by Eva Figes (Pandora, 1993); Youth Clubs UK for Samantha Studley: 'My Mam's Death' from *True to Life: Writings by Women* edited by Susan Hemmings (Sheba), an anthology of winning entries to 1985 National Association of Youth Clubs writing competition.